D0106827

Discovering Your Soul's Purpose

BY MARK THURSTON

From Techniques Described in the
Edgar Cayce Readings and Other Systems
of Spiritual Transformation

ASSOCIATION FOR
RESEARCH AND
ENLIGHTENMENT

A.R.E. Press   •   Virginia Beach   •   Virginia

ISBN 87604-157-8

11th Printing, November 1996

Printed in the U.S.A.

CONTENTS

ACKNOWLEDGEMENTS

Like almost any book, this one is the product of many people's efforts. As author, I have been a collector and compiler of ideas and experiences. The creative side of my job has been to synthesize the variety of outlooks and principles which have been offered to me. I want to thank my many friends for helping me to shape the concepts in this book. Sometimes it was through the sharing of an idea about the soul and its search for purpose and meaning. More often it was the sharing of an actual experience related to discovering a talent or finding a new aspect of that friend's personal mission.

My interest in the topic of this book is fundamentally a matter of my desire and need to know the purpose for my own life. That is not to say that I have yet found that purpose in its fullness. But the principles which I propose in this book are ones which I have applied in my own life, and they are ones which I know work. It is possible slowly but surely to gain insight into a mission or sense of meaning for which one was born.

It has been true for me in that search, as I suspect it will be true for you, the reader, in your search, that nothing is more important than the loving support and nurturance of friends and family. It is a risky and scary business at times to experiment with life and to discover, usually by trial and error, where one's talent and fulfillment lie. No blessing has been greater in my life than to have people who have encouraged me in that kind of exploration and who stood behind me even when I had just failed at something and found where my talents and mission did not lie.

My thanks go especially to two people who have always supported in this fashion my journey and search. My parents Marion and Stanley have helped me in ways that I appreciate more and more with time. Perhaps it is because I am now a parent myself that I can see the special kind of love which is required to not only *let* but even *help* others struggle for themselves and find the selves they were born to be.

v

Perhaps this is the kind of support that we are meant to offer others, not just our own children or the members of our families. Every soul with which we come in contact today is one who is looking for that sense of personal purpose buried within. It is our challenge and our blessed opportunity to support and nurture others in their discovery process. As a byproduct of that loving encouragement, we shall find that we have taken a big step in the direction of finding and living our own missions in life.

Discovering Your Soul's Purpose

"All esotericism teaches that in order to go up you have to go down, and no one understands what this means: to get more you must go down, and to get less you go in the same way as you always go— your Being transmits your life. If you have nothing at present that satisfies you completely, it is because of the state of your Being, and you will never get what you want as long as your Being is tuned in to that wavelength. You have to change yourself to get new influences, and changing yourself is always 'getting rid of yourself'. . .

"If you try to increase yourself as you are, you will only become worse than you are at present. The development of Real Will consists of feeling new influences."

Excerpt from *Psychological Commentaries on the Teachings of Gurdjieff and Ouspensky,* by Maurice Nicoll, M.D.

"The reason why we are disenchanted with ourselves is because we entertain in the depths of our psyche a kind of vision—an anticipated vision of what we could be if we would be what we might be."

Sufi master Pir Vilayat Khan, in a lecture, October 15, 1983

"In my own notes I had at first labeled this defense [the 'Jonah Complex'] 'the fear of one's own greatness' or 'the evasion of one's destiny' or 'the running away from one's own best talent'. . . It is certainly possible for most of us to be greater than we are in actuality. We all have unused potentialities or not fully developed ones. It is certainly true that many of us evade our constitutionally suggested vocations. . .So often we run away from the responsibilities dictated (or rather suggested) by nature, by fate, even sometimes by accident, just as Jonah tried in vain to run away from his fate." Excerpt from *The Farther Reaches of Human Nature* by Abraham Maslow

Introduction

You were born into this life for a purpose. "For, each soul enters with a mission," is the way the psychic readings of Edgar Cayce put it. "...we all have a mission to perform." (3003-1)

That purpose and the living of it is something within your grasp; it is something which can be discovered and applied. Your soul's purpose is the very thing which will give your life a sense of fulfillment.

The title for this book is carefully chosen. The initial word "discovering" is probably the most important one because your relationship to your life's mission is fundamentally an ongoing process of finding and revelation. In other words, there is a dynamic, unfolding characteristic to the purposefulness that you have chosen by incarnating. Your soul's purpose is not something that is found once and for all and can then be "put in the trophy case" for all to admire. Instead, you should expect that throughout your life there is always the opportunity to be discovering more about your mission—some new characteristic of it or some new phase of it that is now ready to be lived.

This book is a collection of tools, techniques and perspectives. It is a collage of ideas, each of which may have a stimulating effect on your thinking processes. That is, you may find yourself saying from time to time as you read, "That's an interesting idea." However, if you engage the ideas of this book merely at a rational, analytical level, they are unlikely to lead to a discovery of soul's purpose.

Instead, what is needed is an active application of the principles which you will find here. If this book is to serve as a catalyst for your discovery of a life's mission, then you must proceed through these pages slowly. Especially in the middle one-third of the book you will encounter specific exercises in self-reflection and inner searching which will take time.

Fundamentally, this book addresses a question that most all of us ask periodically in our lives: What am I to be? We wonder about what the future holds for us. We speculate about the possibility of something which might make our lives special, that would allow us to stand out in some unique way. It is not that we insist out of vanity to be better than everyone else. Instead, it is a natural and wonderful impetus from deep within the soul, from a place within us that knows the incredible splendor of individuality.

However, the question "What am I to be?" is not one that can be quickly or easily answered. Instead, you must begin by asking "Who am I now?" because your ignorance of your present self is to a large extent the primary barrier which keeps you from your destiny. In this sense, you must learn how to stop being the "old" (i.e., the old self-identity, the old ways of reacting to life, etc.) in order to clear the way for the emergence of "what is to be."

This principle is often presented in the Cayce readings. In speaking of mankind's natural desire to know about the future, we are counseled in this material that it is just as important to know from whence we have come—our roots, physically and psychologically—as it is to know where we are headed.

The same principle is illustrated in the way in which Cayce gave lessons for the spiritual development growth curriculum known as "A Search for God." These 130 readings, given over an eleven-year period to a dedicated group of seekers, constitutes an especially cohesive and systematic statement of how to find and live one's purpose in life. There is a wisdom to the order in which concepts are presented (as we would expect from any insightfully planned curriculum). Here we find that the sections on finding one's destiny are preceded by many lessons which create a solid foundation. Among the most important of these early lessons are those on the theme of "Know Thyself."

A final introductory comment about source material is also appropriate. Although any topic can be viewed from a single perspective, it is only when perception is enlarged to include a second or third point of view that stereoscopic vision or depth perception can emerge. This is true not only for the literal process of visually or acoustically learning about the environment, but it also pertains to our study of a concept like discovering the soul's purpose.

Because we want a rich and sensitive understanding of this

complex topic, this book will make use of several primary sources. In such a "comparative study," we particularly want to look for points of convergence where ideas and techniques complement and build on each other. Such an exploration from several traditions or points of view will allow us to see the human soul and its purposefulness with greater clarity and depth.

One source will be the psychic readings of Edgar Cayce, without a doubt the best documented psychic of our times (perhaps of all history). However, rather than examine this man and his work in terms of parapsychological import (i.e., the seemingly remarkable evidence for his gift of ESP), we shall treat this source material in terms of its extensive statement of a philosophy of life. That is to say, the validity we shall attribute to the Cayce readings' statements on finding one's soul purpose shall not rest upon the psychic accuracy he may or may not have demonstrated in other readings (e.g., diagnosing a mysterious illness, locating buried treasure, predicting an earthquake).

Instead, this source material is worthy of our study because of its quality, its internal cohesiveness and its demonstrated helpfulness in the lives of many people who have used it to find and live their own soul's mission. It is the same set of three characteristics which was used in selecting the other two systems of thought which are drawn upon extensively in this book.

The psychological writing, teachings and psychotherapy techniques of Dr. Carl Jung are an extraordinary resource for anyone searching to find a purpose in life. Perhaps no one has formulated a more sophisticated and challenging theory of the human psyche than has Jung. The process of "individuation" defined by Jung in many ways resembles the journey, as Cayce described it, of the soul finding and living its unique calling.

A third primary source of teachings from which we shall draw in this book is found in the spiritual awakening system of P.D. Ouspensky and the teacher he followed for part of his life, George I. Gurdjieff. This "work," as they label it, has frequent parallels to Cayce and Jung in the area of freeing oneself to live the purpose for which one was born. In fact, Ouspensky is one of the few writers specifically mentioned and recommended in the Cayce readings for parallel study. Beyond this one recommendation, there is no evidence of these men knowing of the work of each other or directly influencing each other.

However, when blended, these three philosophical and psychological growth systems provide us with a very effective inner map. They point to specific processes and steps in self-understanding that can lead each of us toward the fulfillment of a life's calling.

Chapter 1
THE JOURNEY OF THE SOUL:
A PERSPECTIVE FROM
THE CAYCE READINGS

We all face the question, "Why am I here?" It is a concern which is really two questions rolled into one.

First, we are asking why souls in general are here in materiality. What is the cosmic scheme of things that brought or placed humankind on earth? This first question asks about universal principles. It is a question that should have a similar answer for everyone because we are all part of the same human family. Our ways of understanding that common answer may vary because we have a variety of cultural and religious backgrounds, but its theme and essence should be archetypical.

Second, we are asking about our own, unique lives. The individual wonders, "What makes me special; what makes my life different from the lives of everyone else here?" We speculate and even hope that there was some unique plan in our being born. It is not so much a plan that our parents may have had (although it is natural to hope that one was a "wanted child"); rather, it is a plan whose source is envisioned as God or one's own soul. And so, the question is expressed as, "Did God send me here intending a particular mission?" or "Did my own soul-self choose these very circumstances with the hope of accomplishing something very specific?"

The two aspects of this question also relate to the way the human being needs seemingly contradictory forms of meaning to feel fulfillment in life. On the one hand, each of us needs to feel a part of a great meaning and purpose that links us in a common journey. We want our own soul's purpose to have a communal quality to it—something that relates to all of humanity. But on the other hand, we don't want to get lost in the crowd. None of us really wants to feel that he or she is just another small wheel in a big machine—and a quite replaceable wheel at that!

It seems that especially in times of change the question of finding one's purpose in life becomes a focused and painful problem. When values, roles and events are in a constant state of flux, something in us particularly needs a constant point of reference—and no point of reference is more assuring than to know what one is here to do.

What is it about changing times that brings this issue to the surface in people's minds? Largely, it is the result of the old, familiar roles of life no longer being functional. It is easy for a society to slip into a posture of encouraging—even requiring—the individual to accept the sense of life purpose which roles provide. For example, for generations the individual has been able to define a life's mission in terms of such statements as, "I am a mother" or "I am a company man" or "I am a public servant." These labels and others like them once had a clearly defined meaning, and the majority of people allowed their sense of life purpose to be shaped by them.

Times of change do many things to a society, and few would doubt that today we live in a period of history unprecedented for the rapidity with which new ways of living emerge. One of the primary results is that it is no longer clear what the traditional role labels mean. In light of the women's movement, which gained great momentum in the 1970s, what does it now mean to be a mother or a wife? Certainly, there are still many people who are mothers and wives, but now those roles are lived with incredible diversity. The label itself no longer comes with a packaged set of meanings. In a scary—yet hopeful and exciting—way, a woman must find within herself the sense of mission and purpose for her life in those roles.

Similarly, what does it mean any more to be a "company man"? Consider the impact of such recent events as massive layoffs and unemployment, plus dubious or even criminally unethical behavior on the part of some corporate leaders. How do these kinds of influences affect the man whose inclination is to define his mission in life as a company job? Can such people maintain their high personal ideals and still identify so strongly with their employer? Can they honestly make a lifetime commitment to an organization if the commitment is not reciprocated? Certainly, in times of change, people still have vocations, but the vocational label itself or the company name itself no longer comes with a packaged set of meanings. The purpose and meaning has to be found or even created individual by individual.

The Legacy of the Cayce Readings

One the richest heritages the psychic readings of Edgar Cayce left to the seeker is the philosophy of the soul's purpose. Second in significance, perhaps, only to the health or physical readings are the so-called "life readings." Some 2,500 in number, they offered psychological and spiritual counsel to individuals looking for a deeper sense of meaning and purpose in life.

In a life reading, the source of the Cayce material would typically include several categories of advice, recommendation and encouragement. There was a section in which the essential elements of the temperament and personality were described. A special emphasis was placed on identifying strengths and weaknesses. A portion of the reading would describe certain past-life scenarios—an attempt to use the theory of reincarnation to define talents and shortcomings within the soul and to provide useful images for understanding the origin of current problems and opportunities. And often there was a section which described other influences which might affect the soul in this lifetime (e.g., astrological influences).

Nevertheless, as helpful as this kind of counsel may have been to the person in search of a life purpose, we might well ask whether or not these readings have any relevance to our own search today. Not only were the life readings given 40, 50, even 60 years ago, but also they were designated specifically for other people and contained statements and advice custom-tailored to them. How could these readings really assist us today, beyond the inspiration we may receive by reading about someone else's journey?

Despite these natural reservations, a case *can* be made for the applicability of much that is in the life readings. It is illustrated by a process that is also relevant to the more extensive set of readings Cayce gave for specific people concerning particular physical problems.

Suppose, for example, that over the course of Cayce's lifetime work of giving readings, he had a total of 100 different people who came to him with arthritis. Each of those physical readings on arthritis contains a statement of diagnosis and recommended treatment that is individualized—the reading addressed medical advice that fit the unique "chemistry" of the body, mind and soul for whom the reading was given. Certainly, there would be differences among the readings given for these 100 people.

However, despite these differences, a careful study reveals that there are some recurrent themes in the readings for the arthritic cases. There are patterns in the way the readings described the origins of this ailment and made suggestions for its treatment. In other words, there are some universal principles about arthritis that form the background for each of the readings Cayce gave on this ailment, a background against which he could paint a unique portrait of the individual and the way in which a particular body experienced this illness.

What has been repeatedly demonstrated by students of the Cayce material is that the recurrent themes provide a measure of applicability which extends beyond the very limited circle of those few who actually received readings from Cayce. A person today is not able to get a Cayce reading about an arthritis problem, but the application of the apparently universal principles of origin and treatment of this ailment are likely to be very helpful.

The demonstrated effectiveness of this process goes far beyond one ailment and appears to be a promising procedure for almost any other. Of course, there need to be sufficient cases studied in order that we might be able to distinguish the universal principles from the idiosyncratic needs of that individual for whom the reading was given.

This process of making universal some of the advice in the Cayce readings may have applicability in areas other than health. A case can be made for using this approach with the life readings. What do we find in the hundreds of instances in which individuals sought advice from Cayce about how to find their mission in life? We discover recurrent themes—repeated patterns of suggestions—in two areas. First, there appear to be certain universal characteristics of a soul's mission. Even though each of us may have come with a customized, unique purpose and destiny for this lifetime, all destinies share certain qualities. Second, the best way to go about finding one's purpose may be for each soul to use certain common tools and approaches.

Later, we will examine what some of those seemingly universal themes are. However, for the moment, our concern is merely to clarify how we shall be working with the Cayce readings, one of the primary resources for this book. Occasionally, we shall look at individual case histories from the readings because they are inspirational or instructional.

More frequently, however, our concern shall be to extract the kinds of statements and concepts that were often repeated in the life readings and to explore their possible application in our own efforts to find and live a soul's mission.

The Seeker

What kind of person is attracted to the search for a mission in life? What sort of individual wants to discover the soul's purpose? Most likely such a seeker is someone whose life is generally going all right, but who senses that there must be something more. However, that something more is probably not a new book to read or a new concept to study. The missing element is something deeper, more at the heart of what the individual is all about.

It is a part of you that is hurting which wants to look for a deeper sense of purpose in life. The part of you that is comfortable and content is not particularly interested in change or challenge. There must, in this sense, be a window of vulnerability if you are to see deeper into yourself and find a profound meaning to your life, even a calling to be or to do something very specific. Certainly, it is a painful matter to put yourself into a vulnerable place and, moreover, to stay there long enough to allow insight or healing to emerge. It takes courage to search for your unique purpose in life.

Perhaps too quickly, the seeker turns the question of finding a mission in life into a concern for a vocational label. This journey of discovery, however, is only in a secondary way one whose end result is a vocational choice. It is true that many find a soul-fulfilling experience through their jobs, but the job is merely a vehicle that can allow one to express the mission. In fact, for many people, the daily nine-to-five job is not the primary vehicle through which their mission in life manifests. They may have a job which they try to do with love and a conscientious spirit, but, primarily, it is a means to the financial support they require to live in the earth. For them, it may be a hobby—an avocation—that becomes the more effective vehicle for expressing their deepest sense of a life's purpose.

As a seeker of purpose, you are most likely to be successful if you begin the discovery process by thinking of a life's mission in terms of a quality of living, a spirit of life. You are not likely to be satisfied with that as the total answer, because the phrase "soul's purpose" connotes something much more specific that you were sent into the earth to accomplish. However, the tendency you may be likely to have, out of impatience, is to jump prematurely to specific ways in which the mission may manifest, the ways in which it may take form.

With this tendency in mind, consider a hypothetical seeker beginning the process of searching for a mission in life. In fact, this individual may have been on the "spiritual path" for many years, working with meditation, dream study, diet, and many other attunement procedures. And during those years of such self-study and attunement, great strides may have been made. A healthier body. Periodic psychic experiences which helped in decision making. A more accurate and honest self-appraisal of personal strengths and weaknesses.

Yet there comes a day in the life of our hypothetical seeker when a realization dawns: "I am a better person for all I have been doing, but I am still not fulfilled." The insight that something is still missing sets the individual on a new kind of search. The familiar attunement tools may continue to be part of the life, but alongside them are to be added new approaches and techniques to suit this different kind of task: the search for that mission in life which, if it is lived, will bring real fulfillment.

There is a point at which you begin as this sort of a seeker, no matter how experienced you may already have been with other facets of the spiritual quest. And, at this beginning point, there is the tendency to impatience, to formulate quickly a notion of how the mission looks. You may ask yourself questions like these:

Is it my mission to write a book on parapsychology?
Is my soul's purpose to be a university teacher?
From my birth, has it been my soul's intention to live
    in France?

At a later point, this sort of question may be relevant, but we must realize from the beginning that writing a book or teaching or living in France will not in itself be fulfilling to any soul. These can be vehicles for living one's mission, a form or manifestation the mission takes, but a soul's purpose is in essence spiritual—it is a spirit or feeling about life. Your soul's purpose has more to do with a particular state of consciousness from which you could live your life than it does the vocational, avocational or environmental forms it may take. First, you should be clear about this distinction and begin to experience the "formless" qualitative spirit in which you were born to live. Then you can feel confident that the forms, the expressions, you choose will be fulfilling.

By way of example, consider a man who is searching to find his soul's purpose and does not prematurely direct his quest toward a change in vocation. Through the hard—yet rewarding—sort of work which shall be outlined in this book, it is slowly revealed to him that his mission in life is "the appreciation of beauty." He may be surprised at this revelation and also want something more specific. How, he wonders, is he to go about living that purpose? Perhaps within his soul there is the knowledge that there is a single, best way for him to accomplish it—a particular kind of vocation or hobby. Or it may be that many choices are available, all of them equally good opportunities to live life from a consciousness that appreciates beauty.

Or, consider a woman who enters into a similar kind of discovery process, and it is revealed to her the mission of "sensitivity to the have-nots of life." What she has found in this first stage of success is the one quality of a greater whole on which her soul most wants to work. From amongst all the qualities and characteristics which we might ascribe to divine consciousness, her soul is aware of a special need and opportunity in one area. The soul has come into this lifetime with the hope and intention of living, whenever possible, from that particular place in consciousness. And this woman is unlikely ever to feel really fulfilled unless she is attuned to that. Like the man in the first example, with this initial insight she must now move on to the next stages in the discovery process. She must choose the forms and expressions which shall best allow her to live from this state of awareness.

A Philosophy of the Creation of Souls

Let us first address the universal side of the question, "What is my soul's purpose?" Because each of us belongs to the human family, there is a certain measure of commonality to our life purposes. Why are souls, in general, in the earth? How did spiritual beings come into matter and toward what mission or goal are they to direct their lives?

These are questions so broad in their scope and so beyond our immediate experience that we can only speculate about answers. Modern science tries to investigate the origins of the universe, but is it really pursuing the same question we are asking here? We can look to various sources which we respect and see how they have answered these questions: the Bible, intuitive or psychic sources such as the Cayce readings, the great philosophers. Perhaps the most reliable answers we can formulate are those which are supported by evidence from a diversity of cultures and time periods.

First, we might well wonder whether or not such concerns are even worthwhile. Why should we worry about how souls came into being or how they came to be in the physical plane? The fact of the matter—this line of reasoning asserts—is that we *are* here, so let us get on with finding meaning with what is at hand. Our speculations about events long ago can never be proven or disproven—so why bother?

How are we to respond to such a point of view, one that is admittedly tempting and promises to save us considerable time and effort? One response is to point out that, like it or not, human beings of today are the product of what has happened in the past. We cannot arbitrarily cut off our previous experience, dismissing it with a wave of the hand and the affirmation, "What's done is done." If we accept the notion of reincarnation, then the soul record from the past profoundly influences how we go about the search for meaning and purpose in the current lifetime. Even if we do not accept reincarnation (e.g., the traditional Judeo-Christian mind set of Western culture), the man or woman of today still must be seen as a product of the past—a genetic, biological history, a cultural and intellectual history, and (if Jung is correct) a psychic heredity via the collective unconscious mind.

No, we cannot pursue just one side of the coin in the search to discover our soul's purpose. If we wish to discover a mission in all the possible richness and depth of that experience, we must work with a dual perspective. There certainly may be that personal, unique calling—what we are specifically here to do in this particular lifetime. But there is a broader context that relates the individual's mission in a single lifetime to a cosmic plan of evolution.

What *do* ancient myths, the Bible, psychic readings, philosophers and other sources have to say about the creation of humanity? The ideas and proposed systems of thought on this topic are vast, but they are not without parallels. There is a risk of oversimplifying an issue this deep and this important,

8

but—broadly speaking—we can identify two recurrent themes in various accounts of creation and the coming of souls into the earth. We can examine two fundamental approaches in creation myths and philosophies.

This is like saying that there are two principal political parties in America today: the Republicans and the Democrats. As soon as we say this, however, an objection comes to mind: A Democrat from Massachusetts differs from a Democrat from Texas. While this is true, we can argue that, despite their differences, they share a common point of view on certain fundamental issues—they have some common political *ideals,* even if they differ on some political *ideas.* A second objection comes to mind: There are definitely other parties besides the Democrats and Republicans. Yet, while this is obviously true, it does not contradict the fact that the Republican and the Democratic parties have the largest representations. That does not make either of them necessarily right or best—but it surely does make their respective points of view worth considering.

No analogy is a perfect fit to the point one is trying to make, but in many ways the example of the political parties is like our study of creation philosophies. Two broad themes or categories emerge from a comparative study. Certainly, there are individual differences among the myths and philosophies that are lumped into a single category. And, certainly, there are other categories than just these two. (Many a reader will no doubt formulate a third creation story category.) Nevertheless, the contrast between these two categories is highly significant and particularly important to our study of finding one's soul purpose.

The first creation story can be described in terms of the following general outline. A long, long time ago—perhaps farther back than we can really count time—God created souls. All souls now involved in the process of spiritual evolution in this solar system were created then. They were made in such a way that three primary components to their makeup were formed: spirit (that is, access to the divine life force), mind (the creative, formative principle by which souls could build with the life force), and will (that which gave them individuality and the freedom with which to create).

These souls were created one with God; everything was perfect. But since God had granted free will, there was the possibility that souls might choose to set themselves apart from attunement and alignment with God. In fact, this is exactly what some did. They perceived that other divine creations were available to them for experiencing. There was, for example, the very limited, three-dimensional state called the earth plane, where a physical evolution of minerals, plants and animals was occurring. A group of souls—a rather large group at that—used their free will to set themselves apart from God's plan, and they got involved in physical matter.

This involvement was produced by projecting consciousness into the realm of the physical; first, directly into mineral, plant and animal forms that were already here and, later, into forms of their own creation. Over a period of thousands of years these souls became more and more enmeshed in the three-dimensional physical plane. They forgot their divine heritage. They came to identify more and more with their earthly experiences.

The bodies of the species *Homo sapiens,* which was the product of natural evolution, became the most appropriate vehicles for these souls' projections into matter. The sensitivities and capabilities of this species offered the best opportunity to get free of what had now become a burdensome and painful entrapment in matter. But even the incarnation of the soul's consciousness in human form did not promise liberation. Upon the death of the physical man, the soul was drawn back again to the earthly plane because of its memory patterns of desire, emotion and attitude. Reincarnation and karma came to be the universal laws which controlled the souls' experiences.

The goal, then, is to get free, to re-establish what existed in the beginning: oneness with God. Things were perfect in the beginning, but the misuse of free will led to a Fall, and now souls must use their free will properly to return to a state which they once had.

This first story may be a familiar one. Except for the concept of reincarnation (and perhaps also with the exception of the notion of souls existing before their physical birth), this story resembles what is taught in traditional Christianity. It is also the most frequent interpretation given to the readings of Edgar Cayce on creation. However, there is another category of creation myth and another interpretive perspective on these readings.

The second creation story begins as did the first: the creation of souls with the components of spirit, mind and will. Again, we could say that the souls were created in a state of oneness with

God. But here the second story departs from the first. Even though the souls were one with God, they did not know it: It was a kind of unconscious oneness. "Unconscious oneness" might be likened to a non-self-reflective state of total absorption in something bigger than oneself. We might, for example, equate it with the sort of oneness an infant may feel with his or her mother: The infant is in an oceanic blend of energy and identity, and it is not clear where baby ends and mother begins.

Although this created state of unconscious oneness with God had in it an expression of perfection, it was not the end product of what God intended or wanted. In this second mythic story, we can say that God's creation of souls was just the starting point of a process, a spiritual evolution toward what He/She really desired. The goal, the hoped-for end product, is that each soul be a conscious, co-creative companion with God. For this to be accomplished, each soul was required to move beyond the oceanic, unconscious oneness with the Divine into a fully awakened realization of its uniqueness and individuality. As beautifully put in the Cayce readings, "each soul is to know itself to be itself [that is, fully awaken to our uniqueness as a spiritual creation] yet one with that Creative Force [that is, to experience simultaneously our oneness with God]." (1210-1)

No doubt, it is difficult for our logical, linear minds to comprehend the paradoxical quality of the goal in this second mythic story. We wonder, "How can I be my unique, individual self and at the same time be fully a part of something bigger than myself?" Despite the limitations of rational analysis, however, we can probably intuit or feel how such a paradoxical state of affairs could be possible.

With the goal in mind, we are left to wonder how this condition was to be accomplished. In the first story there was no such problem. Once God had created souls, everything was just as it was intended to be. The need for a plan emerged in the first story only after souls had misused their free will and gotten themselves into a mess, thereby creating the "goal" of returning to what they once had. However, in this second story there is an immediate need for some kind of plan, because God has only gotten things moving by creation.

If we could be so bold—even audacious—as to imagine the divine mind and its intention, it might have gone something like this: After creation, souls needed to experience their individuality. They already had the state of divine mind because they were one with God, but the will—the very principle which would give each soul a self-reflective sense of its uniqueness—was asleep. It was only a potential, a divinely bestowed gift that was still lying wrapped and unopened.

God's plan, then, was to set before the soul a series of occurrences by which it would experience its individuality—even, we might say, its separateness from God, or at least its capacity to feel separate from God. This was to be accomplished by nudging the soul toward experiences in more limited dimensions of consciousness. In other words, divine, infinite mind was too overwhelming to the unawakened will; so, in order that individuality (will) might awaken, a temporary movement into limited dimensions of mind was planned.

One of the steps in this cosmic curriculum was three-dimensional consciousness, one of the limited states of mind that offered great opportunities in the soul's evolutionary plan. However, for most souls, it was this stage in the curriculum in which something went wrong; there was a departure from the plan. If we liken this plan to the grades in elementary and secondary education, it was as if souls got stuck in the sixth grade and remained there for a long time. Or if we liken it to a cross-country bus tour, the Grand Canyon was to be one temporary stopover because of its educative and inspirational qualities, but many got off the bus there and have yet to get back on.

Once souls entered into three-dimensional consciousness, they began to use their free will to create thought-form images that served merely to distract them or to satisfy confused aims. There was, even in this second story, a Fall; but it was not at the point that the first story indicates (i.e., in a moving away from total oneness with God in the first place). Instead, we could say that the Fall was in a forgetting or a misunderstanding or a rebellion. Like the first story, all of these experiences led to a kind of entrapment whereby the soul is continually drawn back into the earth plane through the process of reincarnation.

But what does this second creation myth suggest to us? Simply that the purpose and the goal remain the same. We are meant to become something better than we were at creation: a higher order of perfection—"higher" because we will have qualities of conscious co-creativity with God that were not possible at the beginning. In other words, our coming into the earth plane had profound purposefulness. We were meant to experience the three-dimensional physical plane—admittedly, not in the way we have ended up, but that is not the fault of the earth or of the human body.

Our entrance into the earth was part of a divinely inspired curriculum to awaken the soul's individuality. We had a work to do here that we have forgotten, but the opportunity is timeless and still stands before us. Our work was not to free ourselves from matter, so much as it was (and is) to awaken more fully to our real spiritual identity *and* to bring into the earth plane the very qualities of that spiritual identity. In other words, it is a work to make finite the Infinite, to give personalized expression to the Divine.

It is the bias of this book that the second creation story is the more fruitful with which to work, one that gives a dignity to human experience. It says that the soul's purpose at this point in spiritual evolution is *right here*—not off in some astral plane or some other star system. This story certainly allows for a bigger picture than one encompassing just the earth plane. However, its meaning implies that our involvement in this three-dimensional life is not a grand mistake of cosmic proportions but rather something that was intended. For thousands of years we may have gone about it in the wrong way, and we have suffered for it. But a fantastically meaningful and incredibly rich sense of purposefulness is our birthright here in the earth, in these human bodies.

Personality and Individuality

The Cayce readings, as well as the other sources we shall be using, make a key distinction between two aspects of ourselves. On the one hand, there is the personality and, on the other hand, the individuality. The soul's mission is known to the individuality, and it can be lived only when one is in touch with this aspect of oneself. The personality can either serve as a resistive force to the soul's purpose, or it can be more passive (i.e., cooperative) and be a vehicle through which the purpose is manifest to the world.

An appreciation for the role of both of these components is reflected in the Cayce readings, in which the personality is not seen as something to be eradicated nor something about which we are to boast or become too indentified with. It is the individuality, not the personality, which more closely defines our real self.

The readings define *personality* as a manifestation of what we desire others to see in us. The definition suggested by

Ouspensky and Gurdjieff, which we shall study more carefully later, complements the one given by Cayce. They describe the personality as being made up of patterns of behavior, thinking, and feeling which we have taken on from others. That is, your personality can be understood to be that which is not really yourself but what you have adopted from the social environment, having been shaped largely by your parents, schools, television and the overall culture in which you live. More specifically, the Cayce readings suggest that the exact patterns which you do take on, from amongst all the options, relate to ways in which you want to be seen by others.

At first, it may appear as if this definition of personality makes you a victim of chance in the creation of such a structure and that your luck in parents, school systems, and so forth is rather predetermined. However, working from the perspective of reincarnation and karma (topics to be explored more fully at a later point), we might say that a predisposition by the soul toward a particular personality leads to the selection (or attraction) of certain parents in a certain culture, etc. In this sense, the personality is not the *real* you because it is the *past* and *not* the dynamic, creative potential of the present moment.

The Cayce readings define *individuality* in terms of the ideal and the will: "...the soul's relationship to that as its ideal in the measures of will..." (294-185) In other words, your soul came into the earth with an ideal, an intention to manifest a particular state of consciousness; it is often referred to as a mission in life. But your individuality is not merely that ideal, but a relationship to it. It is here that will becomes the crucial factor.

To a large measure, the human personality functions automatically, a kind of pattern stimulus/response way of living. It makes you predictable. From this level, the workings of the will are rarely demonstrated; however, from the level of individuality, the will is more fully awakened and functional. In fact, it is what is called "free will" that makes you a unique, autonomous soul. In this sense, the will is the "individualizer." We can see why the Cayce readings relate individuality to the will and its effects on the ideal.

In many ways, this topic of awakening of the human will is the key point of our entire study of discovering a soul's purpose. Consider that your soul's purpose is like an ideal within your individuality, something rather uninteresting and unavailable to your personality. And consider that your individuality, the

14

residence of this soul's mission ideal, is also the home of your spiritual birthright, your free will. It is in the awakening of the will that the individuality comes into awareness and allows you to know what you are born to be and to do. It is in this awakening that you shall be capable of not just knowing what your mission is but also how to live it. Because this topic is so central to our discovery process, the final two chapters of this book are devoted to understanding the human will.

What do you know of your own individuality? Perhaps your most vivid encounters with it come from truly creative moments. Just as it is the nature of personality to do things by rote, it is the nature of individuality to be innovative. Such creativity may shine through you in formal acts, such as painting, drawing, sculpting, writing, etc. Or, you may find that your creative individuality expresses in the more mundane aspects of living: a novel approach to cooking a particular dish, an inspired way of helping a child overcome a fear, a creative solution to a problem at your job.

You may also know your individuality from experiences in meditation. In fact, one definition of meditation is the movement in consciousness that causes one to identify with the individuality instead of the personality. Unfortunately, for most of us, many meditation periods are relatively unsuccessful efforts at making this kind of identity switch. The quiet period is largely spent thinking about or processing the fears and worries of the personality. But there may be those moments in meditation, however infrequent, in which you experience yourself to be something quite different than the role you play out most of the day.

Recall instances from your past in which you got a taste of your individuality. Can you formulate a clear notion of what this term means? Keeping in mind experiences of creativity and deep meditation, can you describe this different sense of identity which you touched? Is it merely an expanded, more beneficent version of what you normally think yourself to be? Or is it something radically different from your personality?

Probably the best answer to that final question is: Yes, the individuality is of a different order of being than the personality. This is a difficult concept for us to adapt to, primarily because the language of metaphysical studies we are used to does not make this point clearly. We are accustomed to hearing of the "higher self" and the "lower self." While this distinction may be helpful for some topics (it is even found in the Cayce material), it is probably not an accurate one for the concept of individuality/personality. An identical problem arises with such language as the "big me" and the "little me," terms sometimes used to teach children about aspects of themselves.

This problem of distinguishing and defining individuality and personality can be illustrated with the following analogy. Imagine it is Halloween and your doorbell rings. You go to the door and see someone or something dressed in a dog costume. Dutifully you deposit a treat in the bag carried by this "dog," and then you playfully begin to guess the real identity "behind" the costume.

But in what category are your guesses? Do you look upon the appearance of the dog costume (i.e., what is similar to the "personality") and then guess the hidden identity as something of that same order, only higher or smarter or better? Do you make guesses like "a chimpanzee" or "a dolphin," which are animals like the dog but which are in certain ways superior? Although such guesses seem ridiculous in this Halloween story, they are equivalent to our frequent tendency to imagine our individualities to be merely smarter or healthier or more polished versions of our personalities.

However, a more promising category of guesses exists about the real identity "behind" the dog costume. It emerges from the insight that a radically different order of being is involved. Instead of the costume masking another kind of animal, perhaps there is a human being within it. You might then guess, "Is this really Billy who lives next door?" or "Is this Cathy who lives across the street?"

This Halloween analogy does not directly solve our dilemma, but it does suggest where *not* to look. In your search to know yourself as individuality, you are going to have to shed certain tendencies to look for something that basically resembles your personality. Individuality stands in relation to personality as a molecule stands to an atom, or as the entire human body stands to a single organ like the heart. It is a higher order of being, of a higher dimension, richer in meaning and in relationships.

This principle is crucial if we are to grasp the meaning of yet another concept found in the Cayce material: Frequently (if not always) the influences from your personality are counter to those from your individuality. "For so oft we see contradictory effects produced in the activities of the individuality and personality of persons." (281-51) In other words, influences which arise from your individuality would take you in a different direction than influences from your personality. Since the consciousness of your soul's purpose is within your individuality, often your personality may not be particularly concerned with or interested in those deep promptings.

But what does it mean to say that your individuality tends to take you in a different direction? Is it a simple polarity in which your personality says "yes" and your individuality says "no"; where the one says, "Stay in the job you have" and the other says, "Make a change"? Or is it a matter of something deeper and more complex? It is probably most fruitful to view the contradictory aspects of the personality and individuality more in terms of diagram (b) than of diagram (a).

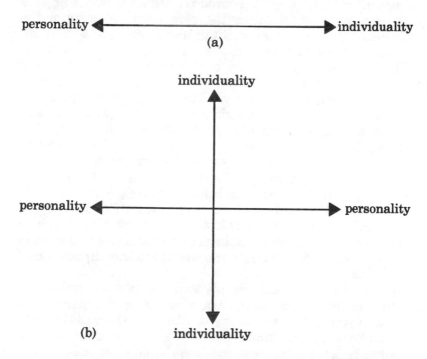

personality ◄————————————————► individuality

(a)

individuality

personality ◄————————————————► personality

(b)   individuality

In diagram (a) the issues of life have a clear-cut "yes" or "no," which involves affirming either the individuality or the personality to the exclusion of the other. But diagram (b) suggests that when you get in touch with your individuality, a whole new set of issues emerges. Awakening your individuality does not make the hard choices of personality life go away. Instead new, heretofore unconsidered, issues come to light.

Diagram (b) implies that even after you add a dimension to your life by awakening your individuality, there are still choices for the will to make. You still have to decide what is best for you at a personality level, *and* you have to select the optimal pathway amongst the options presented to you by the individuality.

The perspective of the spiritual path depicted in diagram (a) is fundamentally different than the one in diagram (b). With the more simplistic, one-dimensional model, it is evident that once you awaken your individuality, or identify with it, the choice has been made (i.e., there is no further application of the personal will on that particular issue). This is a kind of "higher self/lower self" thinking that implies that you are always being pulled apart in your search for higher truth. It implies that once you opt for either the personality identity or the individuality identity everything falls into place and all relevant choices have been made.

Diagram (b) does not deny that this kind of fragmenting tension happens in life (in fact, you can undoubtedly think of personal instances in which you felt torn in this way). But it says that the typical experience of being pulled in two directions is often (but not always) two sides of your personality warring. In other words, many of the inner battles which you may like to imagine as your higher self arguing with your lower self are more accurately described as two sides of your personality wrestling with an issue that is of great concern to the personality and only of minor significance to the individuality. Once you awaken to your individuality, you discover its own unique set of issues and concerns, and you are faced with decisions in another order or another dimension of your being.

All of this is not meant to imply that you have a double-track life that never interfaces. In fact, what you may experience is that once you face the challenges offered by the individuality and make such decisions there, then your choices at a personality level offer best solutions which are much more evident. The mistake you must avoid is to equate your all-too-familiar personality dilemmas with a more profound task: to hear the questions which the individuality is asking.

This distinction of personality and individuality is found in the philosophies and systems of many writers and teachers. We shall see later that something akin to the Cayce distinction is found in Jung's work as well as the systems proposed by

Ouspensky and Gurdjieff.

A contemporary thinker has also spoken eloquently on this matter, specifically as it concerns the soul finding its sense of unique purpose in life in order to have the hope to go on living. Dr. Elisabeth Kübler-Ross is an internationally recognized pioneer in the understanding of death and dying. Sometimes she is called upon to counsel those parents whose children have committed suicide. We should all be alarmed at the rising incidence of child suicide and ask ourselves what causes the sense of emptiness or pain that would lead a child to this recourse. In some instances, Dr. Kübler-Ross feels that the cause is a stifling experience which resembles the tension between personality and individuality. Although she does not use these precise terms, the spirit and meaning of them is evident.

For example, she has described one case in which the mother of an eleven-year-old suicide came to her. She asked the mother what the last day of the boy's life had been like and was told it had been quite "normal." The mother replied, "Nothing happened, he was a healthy, happy, normal child who always did what we wanted." Kübler-Ross's conclusion was that the parents had made their love conditional. The boy had been expected to live totally from his personality; that is, to identify totally with what he had taken on from his parents. He wasn't encouraged to be in touch with what she calls his "own spirituality." Kübler-Ross says:

"'If' creates prostitutes. Because they believe that you only love them if they bring good grades home, you only love them if they make it through high school; and then you add, 'God, would I love you if I could say "my son, the doctor." And you become a doctor but you don't want to be a doctor, you want to be a carpenter. You should be a carpenter. Because if you do what you really love, you will always be an example of love, and you will touch many, many lives, and you will always be successful. But if you become a doctor or a lawyer or whatever because you think your parents love you for it, you will end up shopping for love for the rest of your life. And at the end of your life you will say what the great majority of people say to me when I sit at their death bed, with great grief and sadness, 'I have made a living but I have never really lived.' And to live means to follow your own path, not somebody else's in

exchange of love. Your own path means to get in touch with your own spirituality."
(From a lecture on "Life, Death and Transition," October 24, 1982, in Irvine, California)

A similar concept is found in the writings of the psychologist/philosopher of the last century, William James (who, like Ouspensky, was one of the few writers specifically mentioned in the Cayce readings for parallel study). James' study of the human will led him to a distinction between the "force of propensity" and "ideal action." This first term resembles our definition of the personality, with all its habitual, mechanical ways of reacting to life. The second term resembles the ideal, or sense of high purpose, which is within the individuality.

James then concludes that the force of propensity is always stronger than the force of ideal action, unless the will is awakened and applied. In fact, he says that we can think of the forces of propensity as being directly resistant or contrary to the force of the ideal.

"And if a brief definition of ideal...action were required, none could be given which would better fit than this: It is action in the line of the greatest resistance."
(*Principles of Psychology*, Vol. 2, p. 549, published in 1890)

This reference to the will is very significant and forms a central principle throughout this book. It is your will which allows you to identify with either the personality or the individuality aspects of who you are. It is the will which, according to James, allows you to give *attention* to specific contents of your mind, to specific ideas. But then you are left to wonder just how pervasive or influential your will can be. To what extent is your life experience laid out at birth? Is the purpose of your soul so strong that things are relatively set or fixed from the beginning of an incarnation? And to what extent can your soul's purpose be read from a horoscope or lines on your palm?

The answers from the Cayce readings to these questions indicate that life is not set nor determined, that there is always the opportunity to shape things with the will. For example, one person came to Cayce with a question concerning something he had been told in a reading from a spiritualist. This person asked Cayce to peer into the future and confirm that an elderly person would help him in his life career toward financial success. The response he received in the Cayce reading was "...to say it *will* happen—it can't be done!...depends upon the will of the soul." (531-3)

In another reading we find the issue of predetermined life experience being addressed even more directly: "...it is not that the entire life experience is laid out for an individual when there has been received that imprint as of the first breath." (281-49) In other words, we may be born with an ideal intent or mission as well as the soul talents to accomplish it, but the fulfillment of that purpose requires work and the application of will. We may even be born with extremely strong likelihoods of certain events confronting us in life (e.g., particular people we will meet), but how we shall respond is not predetermined.

Unfortunately, certain signs or indicators of the soul's mission are often misinterpreted as being more influential than they necessarily are. For example, the astrological configurations denoting your birth time may be understood as an outward, vibratory expression of what your soul brought with it into this incarnation. It is more a road map of where your soul *has been* than where it is going. Your soul was magnetized to a certain moment of birth because in some way the planetary energies or influences of that exact moment matched or resonated with the very talents and weaknesses your soul intended to bring with it for this particular incarnation.

But just how much of your soul's journey in the earth is directed by astrological influences? Or, for that matter, by other signs such as palmistry, numerology, etc.? The answer from the Cayce readings suggests that, lumped together, this class or category of influences accounts for about 20 percent of the total. "It may be depended upon, then, about 20 percent as being absolute—and about 80 percent 'chance' or what a body does with its opportunities." (416-2) The last phrase is clearly referring to the human will. Eighty percent of the work of fulfilling your soul's purpose rests with choices you make and work you do in response to opportunities. If you forfeit the potential of your will, then outward signs (like astrology and palmistry) can become relatively more influential, yet you are missing the key ingredient that shall make the realization of your mission possible.

In fact, in the Cayce material, the role of individual choice is placed at the heart of the question of personal destiny. You might prefer to think that your soul's purpose is somehow set and that once it is discovered it rather automatically is played out in your life. Such thinking puts a premium on "discovering" the mission. But instead, this source of information implies that uncovering the nature of the mission is not so difficult. With persistent self-study and openness to guidance, it will be revealed. Instead, your destiny is profoundly dependent upon the difficult and yet joyful work of living out that purpose—making the day-to-day choices required. "Hence, *destiny* is what a soul does with *its* will as in relationship to the Creative Forces." (391-6) Or, put another way, knowledge itself does not bring a sense of fulfillment at a soul level, *even* the knowledge of what you were born to do. "It is not the knowledge, then, but what one does with one's abilities, one's opportunities in relationships to others, that makes for the development or retardment of that individual." (1293-1)

Archetypal Characteristics of a Soul's Purpose

How can you determine the nature of your soul's mission for this incarnation? Throughout the various sections of this book we will explore a variety of approaches; but, broadly speaking, the realization comes in two ways. First, there is the element of careful self-study and analysis. And second, there is the experience of revelation, in which insight seems to be "given" rather than "figured out."

In the category of self-study and analysis, some helpful clues can assist you in matching personal strengths and talents to a specific sense of purpose. Perhaps nothing is more valuable than a feeling for the overall character of what you are looking for. By way of analogy, imagine that you were sent to the airport to pick up the uncle of a friend. Having never met nor seen a picture of this uncle, you are likely to wonder how you can pick him out from among all the strangers you will see getting off the plane. However, if your friend will describe some of his characteristics of appearance, you will have a much better chance. If she says that he is taller than average, has a short beard, and is slightly balding, these clues are likely to direct you to the right man. Although several people may get off the plane who have these characteristics, with perhaps a few erroneous greetings, you will eventually find the right man.

In a similar fashion, there are several repeated themes in the Cayce readings about the mission of the soul. These five universal or archetypal characteristics are relevant to your own search to find a unique purpose for life. It may well be that everyone's mission will not fit all five of these qualities, but the implication in the Cayce material is that some of these characteristics will fit each of us.

1. An expansion of consciousness—a sense of wonder. As you live your mission in life, a constant feeling of expanding awareness is created. Living your soul's purpose will make you more conscious, and with that expanded consciousness comes a sense of wonder and awe. There is probably no better indicator that you are *not* yet living your soul's mission than the lack of a sense of wonder about life. This feeling of life always unfolding, expanding and opening up before you is described for one individual by Cayce in this way: "First, the entering of *every* soul is that it, the soul, may become more and more aware or conscious. . ." (518-2)

2. Service to others—making a creative contribution in the world. Of course, nothing is more central to the philosophy and counsel found in the Cayce readings than the ideal of service. These teachings stress that service comes from the real individuality of the soul—not a kind of compulsive or neurotic service solely from the personality.

The principle appears to be this: You were born with the intentions and the talents to create and to give in a manner that is perhaps better than any other soul. In some special way you are meant to serve others (perhaps thousands of others, perhaps just a few) with a level of effectiveness unmatched by anyone else.

Quite naturally, this principle awakens in your mind the thought that someone always seems to be more talented or more skilled than you. But that is not what the principle implies. For example, it does not say that you are the best musician or the best public speaker in the world. Rather, it suggests that with your unique style and tastes in music there are certain souls that you can serve and help in a way that no other soul could. Or, with your particular approach to thinking and presenting ideas, there is a creative, serving way of your being a public speaker that will touch and lift certain people in a profound way. Speaking of this archetypal characteristic of the soul's purpose, one Cayce reading put it this way:

Know that the purpose for which each soul enters a material experience is that it may be as a light unto others; not as one boastful of self or of self's abilities in any phase of the experience. . .but living, being in spirit that which is ideal. . .   **641-6**

3. Closeness to God. Simply put, the living of one's mission in life brings a deeper understanding of one's relationship to the Divine. Certainly, the first characteristic described above may, for some people, imply this. For many others, the very ideal of service implies the divine source from which all humanity springs. Nevertheless, this characteristic—clearly and succinctly put—is so central to the Cayce readings' philosophy that it deserves to be enumerated on its own.

As you truly begin to live what you were born to do, the accompanying experience is one of directly feeling God's presence. For many people, this comes as a deep sense of being at peace—with themselves and with all of life. For others, it comes as a sense of love; for the first time in their lives they may be able to say that they really love other people; and, just as importantly, that they really love themselves.

Hence the purposes for each soul's experience in materiality are that the Book of Remembrance may be opened that the soul may know its relationship to its Maker.   **1215-4**

4. A view of purposefulness in all of life. Living your soul's purpose sensitizes you to purposefulness all around you. One of the clues that indicates you are on the right track with your own mission is that you begin to recognize and intuit purpose in others' lives. In other words, you must be careful about the search to "discover *my* soul's purpose"; it is not a private search for meaning. Not that you should hope to wear a lapel button that boasts "I've found mine" with a kind of smug, complacent air, but finding your own soul's mission makes you want to help others discover and move toward theirs. Living your own soul's purpose also brings with it a characteristic to help you do just that: It connects you with a level of spiritual and soul forces where you see how all of life is working with a purposeful plan. The Cayce readings refer to this aspect with such phrases as: "For life in its manifestations through which the soul. . .may manifest *is* purposeful. . ." (1293-1) and "For all that is a part of each entity's experience is for a purpose." (1827-1)

5. Joy in life. Living your soul's purpose will bring you joy, a

quality that may not come initially as you recognize your purpose. In fact, to your personality, the mission may require changes or sacrifices that seem uncomfortable or unpleasant. But, despite these factors, something deeper in you recognizes the rightness of that mission as it gradually reveals itself. It is only from that deeper part of yourself that true joy in life can emerge.

In one reading, Cayce gave counsel that is no doubt applicable to us all. The passage states that we need not expect of ourselves some "great deed" in life in order to feel that life had meaning; but rather, fulfilling the purpose for which we were born would bring a sense of joy far exceeding the self-satisfaction that might come from a so-called "great deed."

For Life is, and experience is, what each soul, each entity makes of same. Hence fulfilling that purpose as He may have in thee is a greater service, a greater joy than may be had by him who may have builded a city or have conquered a nation. . .
1129-2

In summary, these five characteristics can be a very valuable tool in discovering your soul's mission. They are the key indicators that you are on the right track. When any or all of them begin to happen in your life in a consistent way, you can be sure you are in tune with aspects of your soul's purpose. They act as important signposts which reinforce and confirm.

A Personal Inventory

As an initial step in finding your soul's mission, take stock of your resources. What are the talents, strengths and abilities which are available to you? You know some of them because you express them in a regular fashion. In the way you presently manifest them, they may not bring you the sense of fulfillment and joy you desire, but from direct experience you know they are there for you to draw upon. Other talents, skills and aptitudes are ones of which you have caught only a glimpse. Such strengths may have appeared in your dreams so vividly that you know they must be an asset of your soul. Other abilities you intuit are within, even though they may have not yet had a chance to be expressed.

Imagine by way of analogy that your soul's mission is like baking a loaf of bread. There are many different kinds of bread.

What will your loaf be like? The resolution of that question largely rests with the ingredients available to you from your cupboard. Before starting to mix a recipe, you would want to take stock of the resources at hand.

Take time now to complete a self-inventory. Later in this book you will draw upon the notes you make in completing this inventory.

Section 1: Strengths, talents, abilities and aptitudes

Review the list below and consider which items are within you. Admittedly all talents are within each soul as potentials, but be more specific about the ones which you feel are especially available to you. Indicate those with an "x" in the appropriate blanks. There are spaces at the end of this list to add others which occur to you.

____ friendly
____ sense of humor
____ innovative
____ articulate
____ sensitive
____ forgiving
____ creative
____ psychic
____ imaginative
____ kind
____ trouble-shooter
____ good with animals
____ good with children
____ good with plants
____ good with _____
____ playful nature
____ energetic
____ logical
____ orderly
____ others: _____

____ motivator
____ writer
____ financially adept
____ committed
____ loyal
____ empathetic
____ artistic
____ leader
____ mechanically skilled
____ pragmatic
____ intuitive
____ good cook
____ industrious
____ wise
____ planner
____ cooperative
____ patient
____ good teacher
____ good listener

____ _____
____ _____
____ _____
____ _____
____ _____
____ _____
____ _____
____ _____

When you have finished Section 1, go back and reconsider each item next to which you have placed an "x." Do you intuitively sense that you are meant to do something more with some of these talents? Even if you do not know what that "something more" is, can you identify some of your strengths which have a special feeling when you think about them? Perhaps they give you a feeling of unfulfillment or a feeling that something is yet to be done with that ability. Try to find between four and eight items which fit this description and change your notation to an "xx." This double "x" will indicate a strength that we will particularly want to consider later.

Section 2(a): Weaknesses

Make a list of patterns and habits of your personality which you consider to be weaknesses and faults.

Section 2(b): Strengths in weaknesses

For each weakness in Section 2(a), see if you can identify an "embedded strength" within that weakness. Remember the concept from the readings that so-called "bad" is merely "good" which has been misapplied, misconstrued, or used in a selfish manner? Although it is not always easy to see a hidden talent within a fault, careful study along these lines can unearth some real gems. Certainly your soul's talents and strengths (ones that are essential to living your purpose) may currently be expressed in your life in the disguised form of a fault or weakness. Although we do not plan to condone the fault, it may be possible to rescue the embedded strength and reclaim it in its purer form. Examples: Weakness = manipulator; embedded strength = motivator. Fault = makes jokes at others' expense; embedded strength = sense of humor.

Section 3: Past moments "in sync" with soul's purpose

List three times in your life which, in retrospect, were *moments of guidance* when you felt "in sync" with what your soul intended for this lifetime. There may have been a certain "feeling quality" to those moments that still makes them stand out: times of clarity or a high sense of purpose or rightness. Go with your intuition or "gut feelings" in evaluating your history and making your choice of three moments, and write them below.

1.

2.

3.

Chapter 2
FROM REINCARNATION TO RESURRECTION: REBIRTH AND YOUR SOUL'S DESTINY

The notion that every soul is born with a mission does not require a belief in reincarnation. We might suppose, for example, that an individual soul along with its sense of unique purposefulness is created at about the same time as the biological conception of the body it will occupy. However, this view is not the perspective found in the Cayce readings nor in most of the parallel sources with which we are working.

Instead, we are invited to consider the hypothesis of reincarnation: a theory of rebirth which implies that many of the tools for fulfilling a life's mission (as well as obstacles that could frustrate it) have their origin in previous lives in the earth. Reincarnation is both a controversial subject and an ancient one. It is most readily associated with philosophies and religions of the East. But many examples of it exist in esoteric Western thought, and even today there is a growing acceptance of the notion in our modern society. A recent Gallup poll found that approximately one-fourth of the adults in the United States believe in the concept.

Of course, the word "reincarnation" often connotes a variety of ideas. But for purposes of our study, it will simply mean a theory of human rebirth which states that after physical death a soul may return in human form, carrying with it predispositions of temperament, interest, talent and even physical tendencies. This notion is, quite clearly, only theoretical and probably will never be provable. As we shall soon see, there is evidence—often very startling—to *support* the notion, but there always seems to be an alternative way of explaining it. For example, even the most remarkable and best documented cases of remembered past lives could be explained as telepathy or clairvoyance. However, we are then left with a problem at least as mysterious and difficult: how to explain the workings of ESP.

It is important, even for those who already believe in reincarnation, to look carefully at the arguments against the theory. However, each aspect of the case against it can be countered with a sound line of reasoning that re-establishes the credibility and applicability of the hypothesis. Yet it is important to know why we believe in something. Perhaps even more important is that, as we look systematically at the case for and against reincarnation, we may find that the theory has often been distorted and used in a way that does not help us discover and live our mission in life. To foreshadow the conclusion even before the case is laid out, we might say that a preoccupation with past lives and reincarnation can divert us from the principle of human potential that instead should be at the center of our soul's purpose: resurrection. But this conclusion will make more sense if we first look, one by one, at the arguments for and against reincarnation.

1. "I don't remember any past lives, so how could reincarnation be true?" This is the most "common sense" case against the whole idea. Yet, it "proves" more than merely the nonexistence of past lives. To adopt such thinking, we would have to assume that only that of which we have conscious memory ever happened to us. This is obviously an unacceptable conclusion. You know you were once six months old because you have seen photographs of your parents holding you as a baby, even though you probably remember nothing from such an early age. We must also reject the counter argument which says, "The photograph is physical proof of the fact that I was once six months old; show me such physical proof of a past life." This line of reasoning is irrelevant because it doesn't address the real issue of the first argument: Is memory itself, or the lack of it, a *sufficient* requirement for deciding whether or not something happened? For many reasons, beyond just the failure to remember being six months old, we must reject memory as being such a reliable criterion. Surely none of us doubts that certain things actually happened to us as infants of which we have neither memories *nor* photographs.

A further point relevant to this argument is that some people *do* seem to remember past lives, particularly in cultures which generally accept the theory. Researchers, such as Dr. Ian Stevenson of the University of Virginia, have documented remarkable cases of apparent past-life recall. His classic book on the subject, *Twenty Cases Suggestive of Reincarnation*, represents the kinds of past-life recall cases he continues to find and study. One example will illustrate how this process typically progresses. It is quoted from a monograph by Dr. Stevenson published in 1961.

"Shanti Devi, a girl living in Delhi (born 1926), began from the age of about three to recall and state details of a former life in the town of Muttra, about 80 miles away. She stated that her name had been Lugdi, that she had been born in 1902, was a Choban by caste and had married a cloth merchant named Kedar Nath Chaubey. She said that she had given birth to a son and had died 10 days later...

"[In 1936] after it had been established that the girl had never left Delhi, a committee was appointed to witness a visit by the girl to Muttra with a view to noting her recognition of people and places... She was...put in a carriage, the driver of which was instructed to follow her directions. These led to the district and the house of Kedar Nath Chaubey, which she recognized even though it had been repainted a different color. In the area of the house an old Brahmin appeared and she identified him correctly as Kedar Nath Chaubey's father (i.e., her previous father-in-law). Upon entering the house, she answered correctly a number of questions put to her regarding the arrangement of the rooms, closets, etc.....Shanti Devi claimed to have hidden some money in another house, the one which was the home of Kedar Nath Chaubey's family. In this house she pointed to a corner of one of the rooms as the place where she had buried the money. When a hole was dug, the witnesses came to an arrangement for keeping valuables but found it empty. Shanti Devi insisted she had left money there and eventually Kedar Nath Chaubey acknowledged that he had found and removed the money after his wife's death.

"Shanti Devi used idioms of speech familiar in Muttra before she had been there, her use of this dialect being a further feature of the case impressive to the witnesses.

"The accounts available to me indicate that Shanti Devi made at least 24 statements of her memories which matched the verified facts ... No instances of incorrect statements are recorded."

(From "The Evidence for Survival from Claimed Memories of Former Incarnations")

2. "Aren't personal characteristics, like intelligence and physical appearance, controlled by genes rather than by past lives?" This argument states that we don't need a theory other than that offered by genetics in order to explain individual characteristics. It supposes that modern science is doing quite well without reincarnation in its efforts to explain life.

Certainly some strong evidence exists to support the notion that physical characteristics—even intelligence and temperament—may have a genetic base. We are all familiar with how this works in regard to aspects of appearance like eye color, hair color, height, etc. Biological research has shown that even more subtle, internal functioning of the body probably has a genetic basis, such as personal biochemistry that causes a predisposition to certain diseases.

But still there remain anomalies—exceptions to the theory which are hard to explain and which call into question whether or not a materialistic, genetic theory alone is sufficient. On the one hand, those who believe in reincarnation counterargue that child prodigies seem to violate simple, physical explanations of human behavior. For example, how can we explain a musical prodigy like Mozart who at five years old was already composing music? Looking back for several generations at his ancestors, we fail to find a similar early development which might have been genetically passed along. Even though his home environment as a young child may have been very supportive of his budding genius, it hardly could be described as having trained him to such a level by the age of five. In such cases, it is tempting to resort to reincarnation as an explanation.

However, another kind of case poses an even more perplexing problem for the sole working of the genetics theory. Consider identical twins. They develop from a single fertilized egg and, therefore, have identical genetic material. Because of these DNA similarities, there is usually an impressive resemblance between their lives—in physical appearance as well as in intelligence, health, etc. Yet the fact remains, albeit an anecdotal rather than a scientific laboratory fact, that parents of identical twins often report distinct differences in mood, preferences and temperament in their offspring from infancy. In other words, despite identical genetic material and fairly similar environmental influences, individual differences still seem to exist even from a very early age. Past-life influences are one way—although not necessarily the *only* way—of accounting for differences for which DNA and environment cannot account.

A materialistic explanation of individual differences (i.e., a theory that recognizes only genetic and environmental influences) is only one of several approaches that can be taken. There are at least three other theories, each of which makes use of the notion of reincarnation.

The first reincarnation option is what we might call a "magnetization theory." It accepts the materialistic point of view but then adds on a parallel, nonmaterial realm of the soul. According to this theory, when a soul choses to incarnate, it is "drawn to" or magnetized to a physical body and a set of influences which resemble patterns within its own karmic history. For example, suppose that two alcoholic parents conceive a child in which, because of DNA influences, a Down's syndrome child is born. According to this theory, the soul that incarnates shall be one which was magnetized to this situation. Because of karmic memories of some sort, the soul was attracted to a situation in which it would have alcoholic parents, and because of other karmic memories the limitations of a Down's syndrome body "matched" its own karmic history.

However popular and enticing an explanation may be offered by this theory, it still has its problems. First, it is dualistic, proposing a physical and a nonphysical realm without any explanation of how two such dissimilar worlds could interact. Second, it has a kind of "have your cake and eat it, too" quality. It does not require biological science to think in a less reductionistic and more holistic way; nor does it challenge metaphysicians with their other-worldly realm to see the human body itself as essentially "of the soul."

A second reincarnation option is a version of what has been called "vitalism." Like all versions, it proposes that a nonphysical entity is a causal factor upon physical development. In a reincarnationist version of vitalism, that "entity" is the eternal soul. The key difference between the magnetization theory and this theory concerns actual *causative influences* upon the development of the child's body. In the first option, there was no such causative influence; the soul is merely drawn to a body and a set of influences which have been created totally under the influence of physical factors. But in the vitalism theory we introduce a new possibility: that the nonphysical soul somehow participates in the shaping of the body into which it intends to incarnate.

According to this second reincarnation option, a hypothetical incarnation of a soul might go something like the following. Suppose, because of a memory of having cruelly maimed the bodies of others in a past life, the soul seeks to learn a lesson by living through a disabled body of its own. Having "selected" appropriate parents who had just conceived an embryo, the soul would participate in the uterine development of its "body-to-be." It would have to work within certain strict genetic limitations, of course. For example, it probably could not cause red hair if there was no genetic basis for such coloring. But it might be able to influence some probabilistic events in development and "steer" things in the direction of the kind of body it wants for that lifetime.

The primary problem with this vitalism theory is the same that we face with the magnetization theory: its dualistic quality. Just how does something nonphysical exert a causative influence on something that is physical? A partial answer has been proposed which makes use of modern quantum mechanical ideas of physical matter. To oversimplify a complex concept, we can say that, according to quantum mechanical theory, any physical/chemical reaction (e.g., those going on in the body of a developing embryo) has a certain undetermined nature. It is probable that it will go a certain way—perhaps even very, very probable. But there is always a set of alternatives. So what is it that actually "decides" and determines a single physical result from among all the potentials? It is a mystery. Some have chosen to call it "hidden variables." Seizing on that notion, the vitalism theory of reincarnation says that, in the case of bodily development, the transcendent soul is the source of such hidden variables.

A third reincarnation option, however, may provide the best counterargument to the materialists. It rests upon a relatively new concept in science: fields. Although we might speak in terms of "fields of energy," a more curious phenomenon is the apparent reality of fields that are not made of energy and yet are still very much physical.

Consider, for example, the problem of how gravity works. This is still an inexplicable mystery, yet Einstein provided important clues to correct some misunderstandings about it. Centuries before Einstein, it was assumed that gravity was an energetic force between two bodies; for example, the moon travels around the earth because of a gravitational force that "tugs" at the moon. But the 20th-century physicist would say that this is no longer the best understanding of what happens.

The concept of a gravitational *field* seems to be a better description. Because of where the earth and the moon are, it can be said that they create a gravitational field that is *not* a force or an energy but instead a "distorting" or a "warping" of the time and space in that region. This is an extraordinarily difficult concept to grasp with our intellects. (No wonder so few people could understand what Einstein was originally talking about! It violated the traditional mind-set that time and space are fixed measurements.) So the elliptical path the moon appears to traverse around the earth is in a sense the most direct or "straight" path for it to follow.

In order to get a better feeling of what a nonenergetic (yet still quite physical) field is all about, consider the following analogy. (Admittedly, this analogy has some inaccuracies. But how could any be perfect in this case, because we are trying to use commonplace items made up of energy to represent something *not* made of energy. But if even the most scientific-minded reader will suspend his or her criticism for a moment, this analogy may be helpful.)

Suppose that John has a longstanding resentment toward Tom, something which John has kept bottled up inside himself for months. But now he has arranged a meeting at which he plans to share his feelings. He realizes that one of three things may happen. The discussion may make things worse between the two of them; it may make things better; or it may leave things about the same. Suppose the meeting is going to take place in a room decorated entirely in red and with a very low ceiling. If the meeting takes place in that environment, we could predict that the chances of things getting worse are 35%; the chances of things getting better are 15%; and the chances of things staying the same are 50%.

But let us further suppose that another option is available. The meeting might have been arranged for a different room, one that is circular, decorated in blue and with a high ceiling. In this second option, we are still talking about the same energies coming together (John's physical body and his pent-up anger mixing with Tom's body and his obstinate defensiveness). However, we are supposing that the energetic reactions might take place within a different set of structures, leading us to predict that in the second room the probabilities would be different. The chances of things getting worse are 25%; the chances of things getting better are 35%; and the chances of things staying the same are 40%.

In this analogy the shape and color of the room are analogous to the structures of time and space. These structures are alterable, as Einstein and others have shown. Fields can do just that. In different fields the probabilities of physical, energetic processes following a certain course are different. Even in the blue, circular room with a high ceiling, the meeting may still turn out badly and things end up worse. But the *likelihood* of this result has been altered by the field.

No doubt, the reader is wondering what all this has to do with theories of how reincarnation works, let alone the discovery of one's purpose in life. In the philosophy of the Cayce readings, past lives and the talents developed in past lifetimes are quite relevant to one's mission in this life. For those seriously considering the theory of reincarnation, modern science's discovery of fields may be an important key for explaining how reincarnation works. It suggests a way in which "soul memories" carry on from one lifetime to the next and that they play a role in shaping the embryonic development of a new body.

Recall that our problem with the two previous explanations (magnetization and vitalism) was dualism: Something otherworldly was purported to be able to interact with things of this physical world. By introducing the notion of fields, we may eliminate much of this problem in explaining how reincarnation works.

Imagine that upon death what *continues* is a *field,* or a set of fields. These fields correspond to many things: the physical body's condition, talents, abilities, states of mind, etc. The fields are physical, *but* they are not made up of energy any more than is the gravitational field between the earth and the moon.

These fields which continue after death are physical, but they will never be able to be directly detected with instruments designed to measure energy. However, we may be able to observe their effects by seeing how they are influential. For example, this theory proposes that the fields provide a structuring of time and space *in which* a body for the next incarnation develops. The fields are not the only factor, any more than the blue circular room was the only influence on how John and Tom's meeting turned out. If there is no genetic probability for red hair or a birthmark or a biochemical susceptibility to arthritis, the fields cannot make it happen. But they can strengthen possibilities and hence pass along a sort of karmic memory—in terms of physical characteristics and temperament.

Students of the Cayce readings will be intrigued by two fascinating parallels to this theory of how reincarnation and karma work. First is the very definition of the "akashic records" (i.e., the storehouse of soul memories) as being written "upon the skein of time and space..." (2073-2) One explanation of this cryptic phrase concerns the way in which time and space are structured as a field in order to correspond to a particular soul memory.

The second parallel is found in the readings given by Cayce on the destiny of the physical body. One passage in particular seems to state quite directly that there is something about the physical body itself that has continuity. Obviously this is not the flesh body, yet the reading proposes that it is still related to it. Fields which are quite physical and yet not made of energy would be good candidates to fit Cayce's notion.

Q-3. What is meant by the resurrection of the body? What body?

A-3. That body thou hast taken in thine individuality to draw upon, from matter itself, to give it shadow or form, see? . . .Hence with what body shall ye be raised?

The same body ye had from the beginning! or the same body that has been thine throughout the ages! else how could it be individual?

The *physical*, the dust, dissolves; yes. But when it is condensed again, what is it? The *same* body! It doesn't beget a different body!   **262-86**

3. "How can I learn if, though punished for a past wrong, I do not remember what I did?" This argument is based on a misunderstanding of how the laws of reincarnation and karma operate. The system is not meant to be punitive nor oriented toward debt repayment. Though it may be easier for us to consider the theory in terms of a cosmic accounting system of credits (good karma) and debts (bad karma), this concept would be misleading.

A more productive approach is to think of karma as memory. Because of certain memories within the soul particular lessons in consciousness need to be worked with. For example, suppose that in a past life 400 years ago soul #1 was the captain of a merchant ship and soul #2 was a deckhand. The captain, an impatient sort of person, would often lose his temper. One day, he became particularly impatient with this deckhand and in his anger pulled a sword and cut off this man's thumb. What sort of karma is thus incurred?

On the one hand, those working with the notion of reincarnation would say that in this situation debt has been established and it must be repaid. They would suppose that in a subsequent life, soul #1 would have the physical experience of a thumb-less hand, either through a birth defect, an accident, or an injury inflicted by someone else (maybe even soul #2 getting even).

But another perspective of karma presents a different hypothesis. It says that the problem in consciousness created by the experience on the ship is the soul memory related to impatience and lack of respect for the human body. Therefore, the lesson to be learned is one of patience and caring for the body. There is no debt to be paid off. In fact, this point of view may be *more* demanding. In a single lifetime of going thumbless, a soul might "pay off the debt"; however, it could take a short time *or* a very, very long time (many lifetimes) to learn patience and respect for the body. But, no matter how long it takes, the learning of the lesson does not require a remembrance of why the lesson has to be learned. Such memories may be helpful or inspirational in the sense of aiding us in having a greater feeling of purpose to life's problems. But, according to this perspective of karma, lack of past-life memory does not block the possibility of growth.

4. "How could reincarnation be true if it is not in the Bible?" To this question we might respond in a fashion which is apparently glib, but actually quite serious: "There are many things in which we 'believe' which are not found in the Bible, including electricity and atomic energy." The lack of some topic being included in the Bible should not be used as a case against its validity. Even Jesus Himself spoke of there being deeper truths which His followers were not yet prepared to hear and understand.

However, some Biblical passages are suggestive of reincarnation or of other supportive principles, such as the pre-existence of the soul. Proverbs 8:22-30 is a passage into which we might read such a pre-existence. "The Lord created me at the beginning of His works, the first of his acts of old. Ages ago I was set up, at the first, before the beinning of the earth." (verses 22-23) Clearly the "I" here is defined as "wisdom." But is it wisdom in general or that deeper inner wisdom with individuality that characterizes the soul? Like so many Biblical passages, it can be read and interpreted in more than one way.

Jeremiah 1:4-5 is a bit more direct in affirming that one's identity and being may precede physical birth. "Before I formed you in the womb I knew you, and before you were born I consecrated you; I appointed you a prophet of the nations." (verse 5) The Old Testament itself seems to end with a prophecy of reincarnation in Malachi 4:5: "Behold, I will send you Elijah the prophet before the great and terrible day of the Lord comes." It was in reference to this prophecy that Jesus is questioned, "Then why do the scribes say that Elijah must come?" His response only thinly veils a direct affirmation of reincarnation, at least in the case of this one soul that had been Elijah: "I tell you that Elijah has already come, and they did not know him. . ." Then the Biblical account of this scene concludes with such a remarkable statement that only the most forced kind of logic could interpret as other than reincarnation: "Then the disciples understood that he was speaking to them of John the Baptist." (Matthew 17:10-13)

In another New Testament passage, clear evidence exists that in Jesus' time the possibility was well known that the soul might have had experiences before physical birth. Admittedly such experiences may not have been understood as earthly ones from previous incarnations. In the case of the story of the man born blind, Jesus is asked, "Rabbi, who sinned, this man or his parents that he was born blind?" (John 9:2) Jesus' response does not focus on karmic blame but rather on the creative opportunity of the situation, and He affirms that the purpose of the blindness is so that the works of God may be manifest—presumably a reference to the fact that Jesus intended to heal the man.

But no matter how we read these and similar passages that might relate to reincarnation, we are still forced to admit that the thrust of Jesus' own teachings do *not* seem to include this theory. Nowhere do we find Him making such statements as, "Do the best you can in this life and, if you don't quite get it right, you can come back for another chance." We are left to wonder how He could have omitted this teaching if, in fact, it is so central to the way in which souls work out their spiritual evolution. One option is that a censor at some point in Church history went through the Bible and removed all references to reincarnation. But, as we shall see, the historical record does not support such a conclusion.

Instead, we are left to consider the essential themes of Jesus' ministry. It seems clear that He was a man more concerned about the present and the future than with the past, so any preoccupation with past lives would seem irrelevant. Although He was very aware of the cultural and religious traditions of His times, He was a teacher of anticipation, of preparation for the end times. Or, at least we may say that those who were around Him and recorded His words heard Him in this way. They even expected His return in their own lifetime. Of what use is a theory of future incarnations to first-century writers and interpreters of Jesus' life when they expected a final salvation very soon?

What, then, do we know of early Church history and what may have become of thoughts like the pre-existence of the soul and reincarnation? Orthodoxy in the Christian faith did not emerge until the fifth or sixth century. For hundreds of years there were many branches of Christianity, each with its own notion of Christ's teachings—branches in Egypt, Jerusalem, Asia Minor, Rome, and elsewhere.

One man plays an especially noteworthy role in this saga. In his own times Origen (185-254) was the pre-eminent theologian of Christianity. Living in Alexandria on the northern coast of Egypt, he was the first to write a systematic theology of Christianity. By his contemporaries he was called the greatest teacher of the Church after the apostles. He clearly believed in the soul's pre-existence; most scholars also interpret his writings to embrace reincarnation. Origen's influence in his own time was great; but, long after his death, we shall see that he becomes a key figure in the battle over reincarnation and the Church's relationship to it.

In the fourth century, Christianity entered the political process of the Western world when Constantine adopted it as the state religion. But which of the many branches of Christianity did he select? It was the version of the region in which he lived: Pauline Christianity. Two very significant influences arose from this event. First, we should note that Paul does not seem to be one who saw reincarnation as being consistent with Christ's teachings. For example, in the letter to the Hebrews, we find this statement: "...it is appointed for men to die once, and after that comes judgment." (9:27) Although most scholars do not attribute this letter directly to Paul, it is most likely written by a person from the same circle of thinking as Paul.

The second key influence arising from Constantine's decision concerns the political infighting into which Christianity was drawn. In the centuries following Constantine, the regional authorities of the Church (called bishoprics) attempted to achieve superiority over each other via theological debates. In other words, a measure of political power was enhanced when the theological position of one city and its bishop could be repudiated in favor of one's own theological position.

By the sixth century certain issues had come to a head, specifically related to bishoprics that claimed to hold positions espoused 300 years earlier by Origen. The emperor Justinian, in efforts that were probably as much political as theological, attempted to eradicate Origenism. At the Fifth Ecumenical Council in 553, certain decisions were reached to ban teachings of pre-existence of the soul. Some modern enthusiasts for reincarnation have mistakenly claimed that at this Council a censor went through the Bible and removed all references to reincarnation. But a careful study of history shows that this is not what happened. However, neither is it accurate to say that in a wholeheartedly, unanimous way the Church rejected reincarnation once and for all at this Council. Instead, here is what happened according to the *Catholic Encyclopedia.*

(a) With the exception of six bishops from Africa, only the Eastern Roman Empire was represented. There were no representatives from Rome or Western Europe.

(b) The Pope himself was in Constantinople at the time, but was being held captive by Constantine and refused to attend the Council.

(c) The Council was not called to deal with Origen, but with three others whom Justinian thought were heretics. The matter of Origen was taken up in sessions outside the official Council. The actual Council focused on a group in Palestine claiming to follow Origen but which, in fact, had teachings markedly different from Origen's own writings.

(d) The anathamas written by Justinian against Origen were for centuries erroneously assumed to be part of the proceedings of the actual Council.

In other words, Origen's teachings, the clearest example we have of the early Church embracing reincarnation, were retroactively (by some 300 years) labeled as heretical. Furthermore, it was done so for largely political reasons at a Council that was not representative of the full Christian world. But before we relegate Justinian to the villain's role in this story, we should keep in mind that by 553 the notion of reincarnation had already become a theory accepted by very, very few Christians. If reincarnation was what Jesus intended to teach (perhaps only to His inner circle), it had been lost around 500 years after His death. For whatever reasons—perhaps because of lay people's reluctance to accept the personal responsibilities inherent in its theory—it was gone.

In conclusion, we must say that reincarnation was not

summarily thrown out of the Bible in 553. Rather, we should examine whether if it was a part of the living tradition of Christ's teachings, then it was lost by a certain mind-set of the people. It is that same mind-set still alive today that must be worked with if we are to find a constructive place for this theory in our lives.

5. "A belief in reincarnation will lead to laziness—an attitude of putting off growth until another lifetime." On the one hand, this rather commonsense objection to reincarnation seems to identify correctly a strong characteristic of human nature. However, experience suggests that this may not be the actual influence such a belief has upon individuals. In many cases, the theory has quite the opposite effect: It serves to stimulate the individual to personal change and growth. Such an effect may be due to an inspirational quality of the entire concept—a new sense of the purpose of life—or to an awakened feeling of determination to avoid repeating in future lifetimes the problems and sufferings of this one. Of course, not all people use reincarnation as such a stimulation to growth. But we can state with some assurance that there is nothing inherent in this philosophy of life that directs people toward complacency and inactivity.

6. "Reincarnation and karma are notions that are fatalistic." Whereas it is true that some fatalists have tried to use the theory of reincarnation to present their perspectives of life, the theory itself does not include such assumptions. To take karma as a rigid law that fully determines our experience in this lifetime is to distort the fundamental principles governing reincarnation. It is a profound misunderstanding of reincarnation to claim that, based on our karma, our lives are predetermined or preset. The very wording of this sixth objection indicates a misconstruing of the laws involved.

The notion of reincarnation can be useful only if it includes a place for a free, human will. The law of karma is best interpreted to say: "There are consequences to be met in *some* manner for every thought and deed." The choice rests with us as to how these karmic memories (not debts) will be experienced.

Let us take, for example, the hypothetical story of the ship's captain and his deckhand which we related under the third objection ("punishment for debts"). There is within the soul mind of the captain a memory pattern of impatience and disrespect for the physical body. That memory can be met and healed in a variety of ways. In a subsequent lifetime (or even later in that same lifetime as a captain) the soul may experience suffering in his own body, perhaps a suffering aggravated by the impatience of others. But, on the other hand, the memory could be met in a more graceful way. He might choose a lifetime in which he served patiently the sick bodies of others, perhaps as a health-care professional. If we assert the central position of the soul's *will* in spiritual evolution, then fatalism has no place. There is always choice *within* certain guidelines of the law. The karmic memories must be met, yes; but the choice rests within the soul as to the form in which they are met and the very spirit in which the challenges are taken.

7. "Obviously there cannot be anything to reincarnation because it cannot account for the population explosion." This frequent objection is easily countered. The very question presupposes a fixed number of souls roughly equal to the number of people populating the earth. It is a rather geocentric way of thinking, not unlike the Middle Ages belief that the earth is the center of the universe. In a similar fashion, some people seem to believe that the earth plane is the central dimension of consciousness in which God's work is being done.

A more accurate description is probably that the three-dimensional state of consciousness of earthly life is but one of many in which the soul can experience and grow. We have a taste of this fact every night when we dream. In the same way, a soul can learn and evolve in realms of experience other than the physical. Yet this dimension is a very, very significant one, full of special opportunities—but it is not the "whole show."

We could *hypothetically* suppose that there are 11 billion souls working primarily in this solar system on their spiritual evolution. At certain times in history, the physical conditions on earth were such that the planet could sustain only a billion bodies. At such times, 10 billion of these souls would have to focus their experience in other life dimensions. The period of time between earthly incarnations, then, might be quite lengthy as a soul would have to wait longer in line for a body, metaphorically speaking.

However, in our own times of population explosion, between four and five billion bodies are physically sustained in the earth. Thus, a greater percentage of souls can be here at one time, and the period between incarnations may be shorter.

8. "Reincarnation fundamentally contradicts the Christian tradition, not merely because it is not mentioned in the Bible but because it eliminates a need for the Christ and implies that each soul perfects and saves itself." This is without doubt the most significant and difficult criticism to answer, especially for anyone who comes from a Christian background and wants to retain the essential values and beliefs of that tradition. The question is most eloquently addressed by Dr. Geddes MacGregor in his insightful book *Reincarnation in Christianity* (Quest Books, 1978), which is important reading for anyone seriously troubled by this question.

Quite briefly, we can summarize the position taken by MacGregor as well as by the Edgar Cayce readings. Although the theory of reincarnation can be presented in terms of such self-perfecting work over many lifetimes, another use and presentation of the theory is possible—one that is essentially quite compatible with Christian faith. The key lies with the notion of grace. Recurrently we find in the Cayce philosophy of reincarnation the prerequisite of divine grace for human enlightenment and salvation. It is stated in several ways, ranging from a theory of meditation (i.e., teaching that we cannot *make* anything happen in meditation, but must learn to surrender and receive the Light) to the very descriptions of soul growth over many lifetimes.

Put most simply in the terminology of the Cayce readings: Jesus is the pattern for our human efforts, for our personal striving to change and perfect ourselves; but that is only half the story, because the *power* is in the Christ. Of ourselves, no matter how many incarnations we may have had, we cannot fulfill our spiritual destiny. It requires a power from beyond ourselves, *even* beyond our own higher selves or superconscious selves. We might say that the entire process of reincarnation and the meeting of karmic memory is working on ourselves so that we can reach a special point. That special point may take many, many lifetimes. It is the point from which we are truly able to surrender ourselves to the great, healing, reconciling Love of the universe. Such a surrender is far, far more than just a mental commitment to the Christ (as important as that surely is). It is a surrender with our emotions and our physical bodies as well. As much as we may want to be able to do that, we may not yet be able. It may take a certain work on ourselves which requires many lifetimes of learning.

The Meaning of Resurrection

When we hear the word *resurrection,* we are likely to think of the central teaching of the Christian faith: the resurrection of Jesus. But we are challenged to think as well of the resurrection of our own bodies. Although some might say that this is a bold—even audacious—assertion, which puts us on the same level as Jesus, a case can be made that it was exactly to such a goal that Jesus' own teachings direct us.

It is interesting to note that the possibility of a personal resurrection elevates the human body to a new meaning. It suggests that the body is not the problem, the body is not that which keeps us from our spiritual destiny. Quite to the contrary, the possibility of personal resurrection indicates that your human body is a necessary ingredient to the fulfillment of what you are here in the earth to do. This is an especially noteworthy principle in the overall study of finding your soul's purpose. It says that your soul's purpose for this incarnation is related to the work of spiritualizing matter, of bringing the qualities of the infinite spirit into the flesh. Your mission, in some specific way, is a step toward personal resurrection. It is not so much a purpose to attempt directly to free yourself from materiality (although freedom may be a byproduct); but instead, your purpose involves an intention to get more involved in the physical plane, *but* in the proper way.

By way of analogy, we might ask ourselves why the Edgar Cayce readings have such an emphasis on healing and attunement of the physical body. Approximately two-thirds of the more than 14,000 readings are health readings. A simplistic answer to this question might be that health readings were what people requested. While this is obviously true, there is no doubt a more profound implication to this feature of Cayce's work. The philosophical bent of these readings points to a central place for the human body. The Cayce source valued and had reverence for the physical because the body was so important to the fulfillment of the soul's mission in the earth, in fact, for the very spiritual evolution of the soul.

We might even go so far as to say that the Cayce readings affirm reincarnation as a working hypothesis to understand our lives; but, the readings suggest that it is the word *resurrection* not *reincarnation* that is the key to our soul's mission. When our focus is that of reincarnation, attention most easily moves to the past (e.g., "Who was I in a past life?" or

"In what other lifetime did I know you?"), and our concern turns to getting free of the earth plane. No doubt the past is influential, and no doubt there does come a point in the soul's development in which it has freed itself from the requirement of reincarnation. Cayce even told a number of people in their life readings that the current incarnation might be the last one required of them. Yet those people do not appear to have been saints. They may have reached a point of relative freedom from the compulsion to reincarnate, but had they reached the culmination of the soul's potential in the earth plane? Wasn't there still a work to do? It is the work of fully spiritualizing the physical body to manifest a lighted, resurrected body.

The point of this distinction is not to discourage you, the seeker after your mission for this lifetime. The very notion of living in a fully spiritualized body seems far beyond the reach of any of us at this point. If you were to assume that you had to resurrect in this lifetime in order to have fulfilled your life mission, it would seem like a hopeless challenge. Instead, this distinction between a "reincarnation focus" and a "resurrection focus" is proposed because it fundamentally shapes the way in which you view life. It is a very influential factor in what you look for in the process of seeking your mission.

The Cayce readings invite you to a journey in the direction toward a resurrection and a mission for this lifetime. While not denying that reincarnation happens, they stay focused on key ideals for a life's quest: (1) that there is profound purposefulness in your being here in the three-dimensional physical plane, in a body; and (2) that your work in the earth is more than just freeing yourself. You are inherently part of a human family that to a certain extent moves together along an evolutionary path. Admittedly some souls seem to progress faster than others, but the advanced ones then have a responsibility to help those who are retarded in their growth. Though it *is* frustrating for those impatient to get on with spiritual development or those who don't really like it in the earth to hear, "None of us is going anywhere until we all go together." But your soul's mission in this, and any other, lifetime is at least in part a work of service to others.

A focus on resurrection moves us away from the natural and yet limited issues of reincarnation:

Do I survive death?

Who was I in a past life?

How can I work on my personal karma?
As important as these issues may be, something else is more important: not the survival of death, but the living of life with love right now; not a concern about past-life identity, but a search to understand who I *really* am today; not getting mired in personal karma struggles, but experiencing the healing grace of God right now. In other words, a movement from a reincarnatin focus to the hope of resurrection is a change from an orientation to the past to one in the present and to your real destiny. It is with such a shift of perspective that the discovery and living of your soul's mission is made easier.

Karma Versus Soul's Purpose

Our exploration of reincarnation leaves us with several key insights. First, the notion of a continuity of life suggests that the mission a soul chooses for one incarnation may be related to the missions from other lifetimes, perhaps even an extension of a previous mission. Second, the talents, strengths and aptitudes which a soul will use in fulfilling a purpose are frequently those which have been developed in previous lifetimes. In other words, we come already equipped to a certain extent with the tools we shall need.

The third insight, however, is both the most subtle and the most significant one. The theory of reincarnation suggests that we all have karmic memories that are self-limiting—so-called "negative karma." These are patterns of thinking, feeling and acting which are based on misunderstandings of life, such as fears or guilts. As troublesome as these tendencies may be, and as important as it may be to straighten them out, we should resist the notion that they somehow constitute our soul's mission.

In other words, your soul's purpose for this lifetime is something which is creative and serviceable—it is something that involves your reaching out beyond yourself. Admittedly, in order to be able to do this you may have to heal particular karmic blocks within yourself. But you should not confuse the removal of potential blocks with the very mission itself. This principle can be illustrated in a simple diagram (p. 48).

In this diagram the label "consciousness of soul's mission" refers not only to the conscious knowledge of one's life purpose but also to the consciousness that allows one to actually live it. There are certain karmic patterns for us all that can stand in

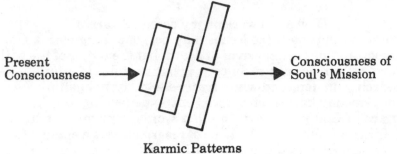

Present
Consciousness

Consciousness of
Soul's Mission

Karmic Patterns
Inconsistent with
the Soul's Mission

the way of our understanding what the mission is and/or being
able to put the mission into application.

The ideas from this diagram are well illustrated in many of
the life readings given by Edgar Cayce. In one instance, an
eleven-year-old boy was told of his soul's purpose for his present
incarnation. The reading was given because his parents were
seeking help to cure his bed-wetting tendencies. The
information first presented in this reading (2779-1) describes
specific procedures the parents might apply (including sleep
suggestion, spinal massage and natural remedy packs). Then
the problem of the bed-wetting is addressed from a
reincarnational perspective and in the context of the soul's
purpose for this lifetime.

The reading proposes that the bed-wetting problem stems
from a lifetime in New England in the witch trial days of some
300 years ago. As an associate minister in his town, this soul
had taken it upon himself to identify children who were having
psychic experiences ("children who saw, who heard, who
experienced the voices of those in the interbetween"). He then
condemned them and had them "ducked" (i.e., forceably
submersed) as punishment.

In the present lifetime, now as an eleven-year-old boy, "the
entity physically has experienced the ducking, from its own
self"—that is, a symbolic kind of self-punishment enacted by
wetting the bed. This is obviously a novel description of the
causes of bed-wetting, which is proposed by the source of the
Cayce readings. We could not assume that it would be offered
for all other bed-wetters, or even any others.

However, what makes this reading especially noteworthy is
what then follows. The reading suggests that unless the
parents help this body to overcome this problem in the next two
or three years, he probably will not be able to fulfill his soul's

mission. If, by the age of 13 or 14 he still has the bed-wetting tendency, he will have developed a very poor self-image and will have so subjugated his own innate opinions and drives that the profound talents of his soul will be buried for this lifetime.

And impressive soul talents are described. There were tremendous creative artistic abilities developed in a Greek lifetime. There were abilities of spiritual leadership, which were learned in a lifetime as a companion of Joshua in Old Testament times. Blending them, the reading suggests that the soul's mission for this lifetime was to be a spiritual leader whose means of expression would be through the arts.

But a warning is clearly given. There are strong karmic patterns which can block the recognition of that purpose and its living. The soul did not incarnate this time so much to work on guilt patterns from the witch trial days as it did to creatively serve a spiritual work. But the limiting karmic patterns must be worked on and transformed if the mission is to be successfully completed.

So, we are left to wonder how this model is applicable to ourselves. We may not be bed-wetters in the literal sense, but each of us has come with certain karmic tendencies that can sabotage the living of our real purpose. Our task is to keep a delicate balance of perspective. On the one hand, we cannot ignore the limiting tendencies we have built in the past; we each have karmic patterns with which to deal. But, on the other hand, we cannot afford to get so preoccupied wrestling with our own karma that we begin to mistake that struggle for the profound sense of purpose in life with which we were born.

The Continuity of Life

Perhaps more than anything else the concept of reincarnation can help you keep in mind that life is continuous. It allows you to adopt an attitude about your life's work that is not bound by the prospects of physical death. Some teachers have even suggested that it is possible to retain a measure of self-remembering from one lifetime to the next, but only if a key ingredient is present. The requirement is a sense of purpose and mission that is bigger than just one lifetime—something so encompassing that a single lifetime allows you only to get started.

Because life is continuous, we can say that the search to

discover your mission is a meaningful quest at any age. The specific purposefulness that would direct you is not limited to a particular phase of a life's span. One often hears older people express a feeling of resignation. "It's too late for me to find and do what my soul really wanted to do." But if life is continuous, this way of thinking is in error. Instead, a person who is 65 or 75 or 105 should realize that at any point in one's life it is possible to start working in harmony with the mission with which one was born. From the point of view of the human psyche—the soul—life goes on, no matter how close one is to the death of the physical body. The dream experienced by a person near death will often give every indication that life proceeds, even if consciousness is about to shift its focus beyond three dimensions.

Admittedly, there are limitations associated with finding one's mission at age 75. It may not be practical to put the soul's purpose into manifestation *in the form* that one might have at age 35. But recall that the mission is primarily a focused challenge in consciousness, and only in a secondary fashion is it a particular way of expressing the mission or giving it form. Suppose, for example, that a soul incarnated with the purpose of bringing hope to others. If this mission had been recognized at age 20, it might have led to certain career choices. It might have allowed special types of service and outreach that are not as easily available if the mission is not recognized until the age of 75. Nevertheless, there are opportunities at age 75 to put this mission into manifestation. Perhaps the opportunities at age 75 are more effectively completed if one has been living the mission at ages 35 and 55, too. But the chance is still offered to do something about one's purpose for incarnating at whatever age the purpose is recognized. The key is to remember the continuity of life.

Chapter Three
YOUR PERSONALITY:
BLUEPRINT OR ROADBLOCK
TO YOUR MISSION?

Our quest to discover and live a unique soul's purpose is enriched by the study of parallel systems of thought. In this chapter we will examine two philosophies which enrich the basic approach suggested in the Cayce readings. The first resource shall be the system of personal change proposed by P.D. Ouspensky and his teacher, G.I. Gurdjieff. The second resource will be the writings of C.G. Jung, especially those concerning the individuation process.

Both of these parallel resources are vast in their scope. It would take many books, not just one chapter, to do justice to the depth of these two systems of thought. Nevertheless, particularly relevant aspects of these resources can be highlighted, and the serious student is encouraged to follow up with more reading. A brief annotated bibliography is included at the end of the book.

Turning first to Ouspensky and Gurdjieff, we should note that Ouspensky is one of the very few writers whose works were specifically recommended on multiple occasions in the Cayce readings. Although Ouspensky was an accomplished thinker and author even before he met Gurdjieff, it seems clear from Ouspensky's autobiographical works that Gurdjieff was clearly the most influential teacher of his life. Ouspensky eventually broke with Gurdjieff, an event that is explained near the end of his book *In Search of the Miraculous*. And modern-day seekers who follow Ouspensky's teaching have certain differences in style and approach from those of today who follow Gurdjieff's teachings. Nevertheless, there are fundamental similarities both in assumptions about human nature and in technique for finding and living what we were born to be. One writer, Colin Wilson in his book *The Outsider*, likens the relationship between Gurdjieff and Ouspensky to that of Socrates and Plato.

George Ivanovich Gurdjieff was a mysterious man. From many of his behaviors we may assume he wanted to maintain that air of mystery. The best guess as to his date of birth is sometime in 1872, which made him a contemporary of Jung (born in 1875) and Cayce (born in 1877). Gurdjieff was born in Russia to a Greek father and an Armenian mother. He, as did Edgar Cayce, had many curious encounters with the paranormal as a child. Gurdjieff started vocational training as a priest and as a physician, but then turned to a spiritual quest that became a remarkable journey all over the world. He traveled and studied in Africa, the Middle East, India, Tibet; and he had a lengthy stay at a Sufi monastery in Afghanistan that greatly influenced him.

After this period of travels, he returned to Russia and began to teach, most frequently in small groups. It was in such a small group meeting in Moscow before the Revolution that Ouspensky met and worked with Gurdjieff. Just before the culmination of the Revolution in the fall of 1917, Gurdjieff and many of his students left Moscow. They had initial difficulties finding a permanent, safe place to continue their work together; but finally, in 1922, they were able to open a training institute just outside Paris called the Institute for the Harmonious Development of Man.

The eleven years in which the Institute functioned overlap, interestingly enough, the four years in which Edgar Cayce had his own "institute" consisting of the Cayce hospital and Atlantic University. Gurdjieff used these eleven years to revise his system of study, self-observation and physical exercise aimed at the reconciliation of thinking, feeling and bodily movement. In 1933 he closed the Institute and for the rest of his life traveled extensively, teaching and starting groups, many of them in America. He died in 1949, still a relatively obscure figure. It has been, to a large extent, the writings of his students that have brought his system to the attention of spiritual seekers in the last 25 years.

We might well ask what kind of person was drawn to Gurdjieff and to his system of self-transformation. The answer could give us a clue as to whether or not we are likely to benefit from his approach. Most basically, the people who were drawn to Gurdjieff were those who were disappointed: disappointed in their own way of doing things and disappointed in their lack of power to do anything about it. They were people who were tired of being comfortable with the old self, tired of being too "at peace" with the familiar. In this sense Gurdjieff's students were generally those who were unclear of where to go next in life or at least clear that what they were doing wasn't really taking them anywhere. Simply put, these were people who were looking for their mission in life and the ability to live it.

Essential Psycho-dynamics of the Gurdjieff Work

Gurdjieff makes a distinction between two aspects of ourselves, as does Cayce with the terminology of personality/individuality. However, for Gurdjieff the words "personality" and "essence" are used. Gurdjieff taught that one's destiny (i.e., one's purpose in life) is contained within the realm of essence. Therefore to the extent that the essence is buried and subordinate to the personality, one's destiny cannot be recognized or lived.

Gurdjieff was fond of the metaphor of sleep. He suggests that in typical, daily affairs humans are virtually asleep. They manifest little or no real will, and instead they live with a kind of automatic, mechanical process of reacting to life with habitual thoughts, feelings and actions. It is interesting to note that the Cayce readings also use the metaphor of sleep in describing the human condition: that the faculties of the soul tend to slumber while it is incarnate in three dimensions.

A key concept in Gurdjieff's psychological system is the notion of many "I"s or subpersonalities. In other words, Gurdjieff pointed out how our personality sense of identity shifts frequently in the course of a day. Each subpersonality has its own set of habitual ways of thinking, feeling and acting. Each one also thinks of itself as the "whole show" whenever it is "on stage" (i.e., has the momentary attention of our consciousness). Each subpersonality may try to be sincere; but because of the constantly shifting sense of which "I" we are, it is difficult for us to be consistent in life.

For example, suppose that at 6:00 p.m. you are reading a book about meditation which is greatly inspiring you. At that moment, the subpersonality that has your attention, the "I" you think yourself to be, is one which we could label "the enthusiastic seeker." In that role you say to yourself, "I'm going to get really serious about meditation and even start getting up at 3:00 a.m. to have a daily meditation period." That aspect of your personality really means it. But in the moment of making such a vow, that subpersonality has forgotten that it is not the whole of who you are. And so, 3:00 a.m. comes, the alarm goes off, but now it is not "the enthusiastic seeker" that rolls over in bed to turn off the alarm. It is a personal sense of identity that might be "the exhausted parent." The intended meditation period doesn't get completed.

Whether or not you can personally identify with this particular example is unimportant. No doubt you can think of several examples that are relevant from your own life. They would be instances in which a shifting sense of personal identity results in intentions not being followed. It is this very phenomenon that Gurdjieff felt was a critical obstacle to the fulfillment of one's destiny. In other words, as long as it is your personality that controls you, instead of your essence, you are incapable of living your mission in life. The recognition of that mission is impossible because its realm—the essence—is buried. And furthermore, even if you knew what your mission was, you couldn't live it. Being under the control of your personality means you are subject to the capricious shifts of many "I"s. From one hour to the next you have a different sense of who you are. And that kind of fragmentation, that lack of a consistent "I," makes persistent, dependable work toward your mission inconceivable.

The work therefore is two-fold. First, it is to deeply recognize what is going on. It is to clearly see the nature of your many subpersonalities and how they control you in a mechanical way. Then second, the work is to begin to build a consistent sense of your real identity, the feeling of "I" that is not rooted in the habits of personality, but is sympathetic to the mission or destiny with which you were born.

A primary tool in both phases of this work is self-observation. Through a careful, systematic approach to self-observation you can recognize the control that mechanical personality has had on you. Such recognition is the first step toward freedom. And with persistence you can reach the goal of self-observation: "to remember yourself." This kind of self-remembering is an identification with the real self, with the essence instead of the personality.

The problem you face according to the Gurdjieff/Ouspensky system is the condition of habit and mechanicalness which controls you. But even more, the problem is your own unconsciousness of the whole process. If you can only begin to understand what controls and directs you, great strides will have been made toward changing things. The technique of self-observation is perhaps the best tool to accomplish this. Something very similar seems to have been recommended in the Cayce readings. In the *A Search for God* material there is found the suggestion to learn the process of standing aside and watching self go by. Clearly this is not a reference to out-of-body travel, but to a self-observation perspective of life.

What is meant by "self-observation"? Is it the kind of self-consciousness we have all felt in an embarrassing moment? Not at all. Instead it is objective, non-judgmental self-perception. It is based on the assumption that the human mind can work on two things at once, a notion that is frequently proven in daily life affairs (e.g., driving a car and working mentally on a problem at the same time). Self-observation is created by allowing one aspect of the mind to continue with its habitual control of thoughts, feelings and behaviors, while simultaneously another aspect of the mind views what is happening from a detached perspective.

One key with self-observation is to do it with loving acceptance. When you practice self-observation it usually will not be with the intention of changing anything right at that moment. The goal is rather self-understanding and a shift in the sense of your identity so that you realize it is not the real you that is completing this habitual response. You are still responsible for the habits; but only if you first discover a feeling of personal identity apart from the habit do you have any power to break free of the habit's control. And so it is with a measure of loving self-acceptance that this technique is employed. As Carl Jung has written, "We cannot change anything unless we accept it." (*Modern Man in Search of a Soul*, p. 234) Acceptance of a habit does not mean a willingness to condone it. However, self-observation and self-acceptance do realize that nothing is truly changed by unconsciously fighting with a problem or habit at its own level.

The technique of self-observation is therefore a powerful step for you toward the discovery and living of your soul's mission. With this tool you can begin to see the patterns of thinking, feeling and acting in your personality which are lived mechanically by habit and which keep you from the creative potentials of your real purpose and destiny. This tool is, however, one that takes persistent application. It is not something which you do for a few days or a few weeks and then suddenly find yourself living your soul's purpose in its fullness. Most of your unconsciously lived patterns of personality have been learned and reinforced for years, if not lifetimes. It will take patient work to recognize them and free yourself from their control.

Maintaining a self-reflective point of view for long stretches of time is extraordinarily difficult. Instead, you might begin by trying to keep such a perspective on yourself for merely a few minutes at a time. If you are able to practice such a "standing aside and watching self go by" for even three or four periods daily, much can be accomplished. You might even find that a self-directed reverie exercise each evening for five minutes will be a good training aid. Just before going to bed, close your eyes and relive the events of the day. With one part of your mind relive the thoughts and feelings you had during specific events. Recreate in your imagination your behaviors as well. However, with another part of your mind, stand aside and lovingly, objectively observe. With no sense of self-condemnation or pride simply recognize the patterns that control your life. Many people have found that such a reverie practice session helps them to remember to do the self-observation work in daily life as the events are actually happening.

As you become more proficient in this technique you will begin to recognize distinct subpersonalities which control you during the day. Some of the subpersonalities will not come as a surprise, but you may be surprised to learn through self-observation the nature of the patterns of thinking, feeling and acting that are distinctive to each subpersonality. And as your proficiency in this technique further develops you will find that the "I" which is doing the self-observation is the "I" of your essence—it is from the perspective of your individuality that you perceive the patterns of your personality. This for Gurdjieff is the moment of having "remembered yourself."

The Human Personality as a Wheel

A visual image may help you get a clearer sense of what Gurdjieff meant by the personality. Consider the metaphor of a wheel. If you are on the rim of a wheel it gives the feeling of movement toward a goal, but in the end it merely brings you back to the point from which you began. In the same fashion, your personality will often appear to lead you in new directions only to bring you back to the same issues or problems in life.

For example, think of a time in your life when you wanted to make a change in order to get away from a troublesome person or condition. Perhaps it was a situation in which you could not see your own role in the creation of the problem and tended to blame others. And so you wanted out. Perhaps your example relates to a job or a close personal relationship.

Did the change actually solve the problem? Most likely you experienced temporary relief from the difficulty, only to discover months or years later that the same kind of issue or problem was arising again in the new situation, job or relationship. Because something in you had not been changed, you were drawn back to a similar difficulty. Because your habitual personality was responsible, at least in part, for the creation of the original problem, it was again involved in the creation of the repeated difficulty. Since your personality was controlling your behavior, there was a strong tendency to repeat the past. In this sense we can say that your personality is like a wheel: It moves, apparently in a direction away from an old situation, only to bring you back later to the same point from which you began.

In the analogy of the wheel there are many subpersonalities which live on the rim of the wheel. Each of these subpersonalities creates a particular feeling of personal identity. In the course of a day, your attention moves from one to the next, in rather random order. What governs the shift from one sense of identity to the next are the events of daily living: what people say to you, what happens to the stock market, the weather, etc. We could think of these influences which arise from outer, material life as being like "bumps" which keep the wheel turning. You may recall the experience of helping a child enjoy a playground merry-go-round. With the child seated on the merry-go-round and you standing alongside it, you would have to give the rim of the merry-go-round a brief push or "bump" every five or ten seconds to keep it turning. Material life gives you those "bumps." In Gurdjieff's system they are called "shocks." They prod you from one feeling of who you are to another, and in so doing keep your wheel turning.

In the diagram on p. 58 the subpersonalities are represented by the various "I"s on the rim of the wheel. Each "I" has associated with it a set of spokes. These spokes represent habitual traits which are a part of that particular "I" and its way of seeing and responding to the world. For example, if one of your subpersonalities could be labeled "the compulsive pleaser," you might find that certain attitudes, emotions and behaviors manifest in an automatic, mechanical way

57

whenever that subpersonality has your attention. The spokes might be labeled with words like "inferiority feelings," or "volunteers for tasks I don't have time to do" or "smiles a lot although it's not sincere" and so forth. Or, if another of your subpersonalities was labeled "the get-it-done adminstrator," the spokes might have labels like "feeling hurried" or "talks brusquely to subordinants" or "logically categorizes each experience."

It is a highly significant step in discovering your soul's purpose to understand as many subpersonalities of your wheel as possible. The strong tendency which you have to stay on the wheel is the very thing which most directly keeps you from getting on with your life's mission. Of course, this is *not* to say that the personality disappears for the individual who is living his or her mission. What does change, however, is the automatic and unconscious way in which one lets himself slip back into the wheel's control of his life. In other words, the injunction "Know Thyself" is the heart of this first key step in finding your life's purpose. You must begin by fully recognizing the influences within yourself that keep you from being able to see and to live that mission.

Just as you completed an inventory of strengths, talents and abilities at the end of Chapter One, it is now time to do another workshop exercise. This experience involves a careful self-study and a period for recording insights about your subpersonalities. Hopefully, you will identify at least four frequent subpersonalities and give each of them a name (just as we did with the examples of "the compulsive pleaser" and "the get-it-done administrator"). The worksheet has been designed to make notes about four subpersonalities. If you identify more than four, then re-create this workshop diagram on a separate piece of paper in order to make notes on the additional ones.

Write the subpersonality labels on the rim of the wheel in the spaces indicated. The wheel has been divided into quadrants, with each section providing a space for you to make notes about habitual patterns you notice. Leave the center circle blank. We will discuss what goes in that circle later. In the second ring, you can record the automatic responses of *attitude and emotion* which characterize that subpersonality. In the outer ring you can make notes regarding the habitual *actions and behaviors* of that subpersonality. (The worksheet is on p. 60.)

Although many, if not most, of the entries you will make on the worksheet describe rather negative patterns, this is not always the case. In other words, most of your subpersonalities will to some extent make use of certain talents and strengths of your soul. Unfortunately, those strengths may be used by the subpersonalities in a very limited or self-serving way.

Some of the talents, aptitudes, skills and strengths which you listed on the inventory in Chapter One may appear again on this worksheet. For example, "the compulsive pleaser" might employ his soul strength of being able to make others happy. In this case the motivation might be to lessen his own insecurity. Or, "the get-it-done administrator" might use her soul's aptitude for being aware of many diverse things at the same time. But here the talent might be used for the purpose of keeping an overly tight control on things out of fear.

Try to be as honest with yourself as possible in completing this worksheet. You may want to take several days to work on it. Use the exercise of self-observation as an aid. It can be done in a recall/reverie format or as daily life events are actually happening.

Once you have completed the first draft of your self-observation worksheet, you can consider what goes in the center circle which has been left blank. What is the hub of the personality wheel? What is the point of focus around which the various subpersonalities all rotate, the point served by the spokes of your habitual traits of thinking, feeling and acting?

In Gurdjieff's system the hub is called the "chief feature" or "chief fault." It is a core state of consciousness which serves as the heart of your unique personality. It is essentially a misunderstanding of the nature of life, the nature of energy and your relationship to it. For this reason, the term "chief misunderstanding" may be a better one to describe its function and character.

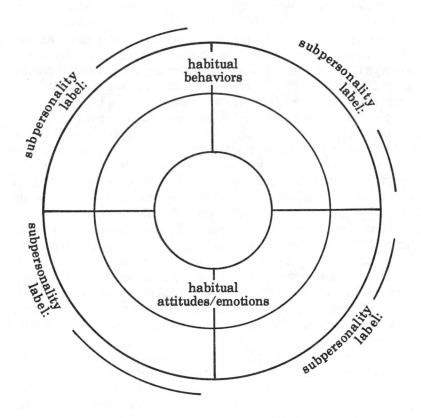

For example, one person's chief misunderstanding might be described with the word "control." His various subpersonalities would all be oriented toward fostering a sense of being in control of what is going on in his life. Because the challenges and opportunities vary from one area of his life to another, an array of different subpersonalities has emerged; but each one exists to contribute to a greater sense of control in life.

Why is this a "misunderstanding"? Certainly there is a constructive place for control in life, both in the sense of self-discipline as well as some degree of influence on what is happening in the surrounding world. But if control has become the central focus of one's life, the very ideal around which one's personality operates, then truly this reflects a misunderstanding of the nature of God and one's own spiritual being. And as long as this person's life is primarily directed by the personality and its hub, there is little hope of his finding and getting on with his real mission in life.

It should be noted, as well, what role the spokes of the wheel play in relation to the hub. Their focus of direction is shaped by the quality of this central point. In other words, the traits that are lived in an automatic, unconscious, mechanical fashion are subservient to the chief misunderstanding. This will be an especially important principle to which you shall return later as you formulate a tentative statement of your soul's mission. Some of those mechanical traits, those spokes, contain significant soul strengths and talents. Because they receive their direction from the chief misunderstanding, they may currently come out looking unhealthy.

But they are still redeemable talents that may be crucial ones to mobilize in living your purpose. For example, the man we have just considered may have a soul talent called a sense of humor, but because it gets its direction from "control" it comes out looking like sarcasm or other "jokes" at the expense of others which allows him to gain control over situations. That very talent of a sense of humor may be a critical strength to call upon in the living of his real mission; however, it will have to gain its direction from some other center of consciousness.

Or, consider another example. Suppose a woman's chief misunderstanding could be summarized with the phrase "life is full of sadness." Her various subpersonalities would all be oriented toward recognizing and relating to the pain and sorrow of life. Again, we might say that even the chief misunderstanding may contain a degree of truth. There is certainly an important place in life for being sensitive to the tragedy and sadness in human experience. However, it becomes a misunderstanding when the personality revolves around this point of view.

In the book *In Search of the Miraculous* Ouspensky tells of a night when Gurdjieff spoke about the "chief feature" to his Moscow study group. He had been working with this group for some time and that night told each member of the group what he felt of their own, unique "chief feature." Ouspensky was told that the phrase "extreme individualism" described his. Of course, there is a constructive place for individualism in our lives, but for Ouspensky this had become a central focus of his habitual personality. It had gone to the point of cutting him off from other people and it had truly become a paralyzing misunderstanding.

Another man was told that his "chief feature" was best described with the words "never at home." Perhaps we can all relate to a part of ourselves that is restless and unable to achieve the feeling of inner peace that comes with being "at home." But for this man it had apparently become so all encompassing a direction to his life that all his subpersonalities served to perpetuate this feeling.

Are you able to get a sense of your own "chief misunderstanding"? Don't be in a hurry to formulate a statement of its nature. It may take many months of honest self-observation to catch a glimpse of it. The more fully you are able to identify particular subpersonalities and their "spokes" the better chance you will have to see it. You can begin to "trace back" the direction and motivation of your habitual traits and see a common point, a center of convergence. When you feel that this insight finally begins to emerge, write a word or phrase to describe it in the center circle of the self-observation worksheet.

Don't wait until you think you know your "chief misunderstanding" before moving on with this book. Keep in mind that the self-observation discipline of staying familiar with your personality and its habits is an ongoing, lifetime work. The "chief misunderstanding" is something with which you may have to contend for a long time, even after you have found your soul's mission and have started living it. There is likely to remain a certain allure from the hub of your personality. Your job is not so much to destroy the hub of the wheel, but instead to learn how to free yourself from its powerful and automatic hold on you. Because, as long as you are primarily directed and influenced in life from it, you cannot get on with your mission.

Carl Jung and the Process of Individuation

A second very helpful resource is found in the writings of the Swiss psychiatrist Carl Jung. A contemporary of Cayce and Gurdjieff, he was born in 1875, the same decade as the other two. Jung's system is largely descriptive of the process of individuation, a psychological growth sequence by which the individual fulfills the potential of humanness in general, and his or her own unique self in specific. In many ways this process resembles Gurdjieff's notion of living one's destiny or fate, as well as Cayce's idea of discovering one's mission or purpose.

It is, of course, impossible to summarize in just a few paragraphs the essence of a man's ideas which is encompassed by some eighteen volumes in his *Collected Works*. The reader who wishes to pursue a more careful study of Jung's thought might try one of his own books, such as the autobiography— *Memories, Dreams and Reflections*—or *Modern Man in Search of a Soul*. Or, John Welch's book *Spiritual Pilgrims* provides important insights on the stages of the individuation process.

Jung first achieved notoriety as a follower of Freud. Some even felt that Jung was his protegé, being groomed as his successor. But the two men split, largely over a disagreement concerning the nature of the human unconscious. Freud felt that the unconscious was exclusively controlled by a primal sexual drive. Jung did not deny that much of human behavior and dreaming was influenced in such a way, but he also felt that the unconscious had a healthy and holistic nature as well. For Jung the purpose of life is far greater than just learning how to cope with maladjustment in one's psycho-sexual make-up. There is also a challenge to cooperate with a profound impetus from deep within one's own being, an impetus toward wholeness. Fulfilling the unique way in which your soul goes through the process of individuation is, for Jung, the highest purpose you have in life.

Jung's model of the mind has three principal components. The conscious mind is merely the tip of the iceberg. It is the product of the interaction of the physical body and the physical environment with the influences coming from two deeper layers of the mind. One of these unconscious levels is the personal unconscious, a storehouse of the individual's memories. This collection of past feelings, thoughts and sensations is much like the subconscious mind in the system proposed by the Cayce readings. A deeper layer of the unconscious is what Jung called the collective unconscious mind. This is a "shared" stratum of the human psyche, a level of mind in which all human beings participate.

The notion of a collective unconscious is one of the principal contributions of Jung's work. He collected cross-cultural research to demonstrate that certain themes and symbols have recurred historically and geographically in a way that cannot be explained in a physical way. The solution he proposes is a level of mind that contains these "archetypal" or universal themes, a collective unconscious to which we all have access.

Among the archetypes which constitute the collective unconscious are ones like "the wise old man," and "the Self." These universal patterns of wholeness participate in an impetus upon each of us toward wholeness, toward the process of individuation. For many, if not most, people this impetus is ignored or resisted. But for the few who want to find and live their mission in life, this impetus is a friend and a powerful aid.

The awakening of the archetype of the Self (that is, the real self) has a universal flavor to it. But it also has a unique expression for each of us. Because that impetus toward wholeness blends with patterns of the personal unconscious and the conscious, it takes on a particular nature for each person. It takes the form of a special mission in life. By discovering and living that mission one is on the path to individuation.

Self-Understanding and Jungian Theory

There is considerable similarity between concepts found in Jung's writings and the ideas from Gurdjieff's system and Cayce readings. The terminology is, however, occasionally different. Cayce and Gurdjieff apparently meant something similar by the word "personality." But Jung used this term in a different fashion, something more all-encompassing and somewhat like Gurdjieff's notion of one's "being." On the other hand, the Jungian idea of the "persona" in many ways resembles what Cayce and Gurdjieff called "personality." In all three systems, then, we find the concept of personal identity (or identities) which are more or less masks for a more essential sense of spiritual identity. Those masks may be learned from the environment or they may be defense mechanisms. But no matter how they originate they can cause a problem for us when we get fooled into a belief that we are our masks.

The Cayce readings call this deeper sense of identity the "individuality," which resembles Gurdjieff's notion of the essence. It is more difficult to pin down a precise Jungian term which matches the other two. Perhaps the archetype of the Self is the closest concept in Jung's writing. This is especially so if we can understand the universal "Self" as expressing in unique ways for each individual soul.

Just as there are helpful tools for finding your soul's purpose in the Cayce readings and in Gurdjieff's system, Jungian psychology has many significant techniques and principles for self-understanding. For example, Jung made frequent use of active imagination as a tool for awakening insights from the soul. And he often asked his clients to draw symmetrical, symbolic pictures called "mandalas" as an expression of development along the individuation process. Jung also developed an elaborate scheme for dream interpretation which was particularly sensitive to archetypal symbols. With all of these techniques, the counsel of a trained analyst is probably necessary to derive their potential to help significantly.

However, another approach from Jungian thought is more readily adaptable. It concerns the notion that you have a temperament which predisposes you to relate to yourself and life in a particular fashion. Of course, many, many efforts have been made to categorize differences in temperament. These attempts range from the Greeks with their four dispositions (phlegmatic, sanguine, choleric, and melancholic) to astrological systems (e.g., the twelve sun signs) to modern temperament classifications based on body type. Jung, however, developed his own way of categorizing human personality.

Jung's approach to self-understanding via temperament classification has gained considerable respect since it was first proposed. It has several levels of complexity, depending upon how many variables one wishes to include. The range is from four basic types (based on what Jung called the four functions) up to sixteen distinct types (created by introducing two additional variables). In this chapter we will deal only with Jung's classifications in their simplest version. However, if you wish to pursue this topic in greater detail, there are many books available on the topic (e.g., *Please Understand Me* by Keirsey and Bates).

Nearly all of us resist the idea of being put in a pigeonhole and reduced to a very narrow description of "who we really are." And Jung would have been the first to admit the limitations of any system that categorizes people. In fact, each soul has its unique characteristics. Nevertheless, Jung felt that his work with people had shown him a distinct number of personality "types," and knowing one's own type had profound implication for self-understanding.

Your personality type describes a kind of blueprint for your soul in this incarnation. It gives the basic outline of your predispositions to see and respond to life. To this extent your mission in life should work in harmony with these predispositions. To understand your own type is to gain a clue about the direction in which your life mission might flow. It can also suggest positive opportunities and potential problems for you as you interact with others in living your life's purpose. Each day you encounter people who are the same type as you and those who are different. This is not to say that your life's mission involves avoiding those of a different type and banding with those of a similar type. Such an effort would be impractical and quite limiting. But you are more likely to be successful with your mission if you are sensitive to the fundamental differences in people which can be described in terms of types.

There is another reason for applying Jung's concept of types to your efforts to find your mission. As we have seen from Gurdjieff's system, one of the primary stumbling blocks in your journey to discover and live your purpose is unconscious hindrance—the living of habits in an automatic, mechanical way. The predisposed fashion in which you see and respond to life—your type—is especially vulnerable to habit and mechanicalness. So, by identifying your type classification, you also identify a function of living which is likely to be rooted in habits that keep you from the creative, serving nature of your mission.

No doubt all of this discussion of Jung types theory would make more sense with examples. You probably find yourself wondering "What are the types?" However, before learning about them, you are invited to complete a brief paper and pencil inventory which will give you an indicator of your own type. The inventory has 54 items and for each one you are asked to choose whether answer "a" or answer "b" best describes the way you are most of the time. Because it is not always easy to choose, there are five options. You can choose "a" strongly or "a" mildly; or, you can choose "b" strongly or "b" mildly. In addition there is the option to skip the item, which means you cannot choose or that "a" and "b" are exactly, equally true of you. Make all your answers on the answer sheet at the end of the inventory. The answer sheet is printed following the questions. Note that on the answer sheet the numbering of the questions proceeds horizontally. Some of the items have been adapted from the Gray-Wheelwright Jungian Type Survey and from the Keirsey Temperament Sorter. At the end of this inventory you will find instructions for tabulating your results.

Jungian Personality Inventory

This is an inventory related to your personality type, not a test of emotion or intelligence. There are no correct or incorrect answers. You will undoubtedly find that on some or many items you find it hard to answer because different parts of you would answer in different ways. Try, however, to respond in terms of your most frequent and habitual personality. This is in distinction from how you would like to be, what you are trying to make yourself be, or what the current circumstances of your life are forcing you to be.

The answer sheet gives examples of the five possible responses you can make to each item. One option is to skip an item which you do not understand or for which you feel you cannot make any other choice. However, the fewer items you skip, the more reliable will be the inventory results. Make all responses on your separate answer sheet which follows the questions.

1. Assuming I try to be tactful, my more frequent impulse is to: (a) speak out, (b) be non-committal.
2. Assuming my financial needs were met, I would prefer to follow a vocation on the: (a) imaginative side, (b) practical side.
3. In making judgments I am more comfortable with: (a) logical judgments, (b) value judgments.
4. In general practice I am: (a) casual, (b) punctual.
5. Mostly I prefer people with: (a) good thinking, (b) good feeling.
6. When reading a book I: (a) often read only a portion of it, feeling I have gotten the main points and skip the rest, (b) almost always read a book all the way through.
7. It is easier for me to devote myself to: (a) social problems, (b) my friends' problems.
8. When I pick a gift for someone, I most often seek something: (a) I think will be a pleasant surprise, (b) I think he or she needs.

9. When my opinions vary from those in my circle, I am most often: (a) intrigued, (b) uncomfortable.
10. When getting ready to travel, I usually pack up: (a) at the last moment, (b) at leisure, in advance.
11. To me, tact is a matter of: (a) respecting independent views, (b) warm sympathy.
12. When it comes to making a decision, I am: (a) very frequently unable to decide because of equally attractive alternatives, (b) usually NOT hampered by equally attractive alternatives and can respond promptly.
13. Assuming I was equally familiar with both plays, I would prefer to go to the theater to see: (a) Hamlet, (b) Romeo and Juliet.
14. If I eliminate for a moment any of my actual life circumstances, it is my natural impulse and tendency to be a: (a) spender, (b) saver.
15. Confronted with misfortunes for others, it is my more frequent impulse to: (a) search for the causes, (b) offer sympathy.
16. When it comes to dealing with practical life details, I tend to be: (a) impatient with them, (b) skillful and efficient.
17. When someone is talking to me I usually: (a) only halfway hear what they are saying because I am thinking of something else, (b) am a good and sympathetic listener.
18. Conclusions most often come to me by: (a) immediate inspiration, (b) practical considerations.
19. Toward goals once chosen I am: (a) tenacious, (b) readily re-oriented.
20. Overall, people who know me best consider me to be: (a) full of high ideals that are often impractical, (b) pragmatic; entertaining only those ideals that are reasonably sure of being accomplished.
21. Assuming secrecy and confidentiality would be assured, my attitude toward a personal diary is: (a) they are a waste of time, (b) they are a valuable way of hanging on to memories.
22. When I find myself being neat and orderly it feels like: (a) a real achievement, (b) something inborn.
23. Compared to how much I think about the future, I: (a) think more about the future than the past, (b) think more about the past than the future.
24. The way of coming to know something that has the clearest impact on me is: (a) generally my inner intuitions, (b) generally physical facts.
25. When I am around small children, my overall tendency is to be: (a) impatient with them, (b) patient with them.
26. I am tempted to new pursuits: (a) quite a bit, (b) only rarely.
27. When it comes to organizing things I: (a) am systematic and ordered, (b) prefer unstructured, flexible approaches.
28. When it comes to dealing with mechanical things or fixing things, I: (a) usually don't feel competent, (b) find it comes naturally.
29. In general the people who know me well would say that I am: (a) not a spontaneous person, (b) a spontaneous person.

30. I am a person who most often: (a) has trouble getting things done, meeting deadlines, etc. (b) is an expediter, a get-it-done person.
31. When facing a decision that will change my life significantly, I most often: (a) collect my thoughts and decide reasonably quickly, (b) am slow to decide and put it off.
32. When it comes to dealing with or discussing non-material things I generally feel: (a) quite comfortable, (b) out of place.
33. I am: (a) not error prone, (b) make a fair number of errors.
34. Overall I tend more often to: (a) see the big picture, (b) notice details.
35. When I think about the past it is more often about:
    (a) the actions or happenings of events, (b) the feelings the events awakened in me.
36. When it comes to developing or reaping the fruits of my ideas and insights: (a) *other* people often reap the fruits instead of me, (b) I generally develop them or reap their fruits.
37. Without having looked at a clock recently I: (a) still usually know what time it is with good accuracy, (b) have trouble guessing accurately at the time.
38. My imaginings are: (a) of central importance to me, (b) curious and sometimes interesting to me, but not of central importance.
39. In trying to prove a point or get a point across, I am: (a) skillful in the use of words, (b) find that words get in my way.
40. My inspirations are most often focused on: (a) how things could be in the future, (b) how to deal with a practical life concern here and now.
41. When I have to change a pre-arranged schedule, I usually:
    (a) get frustrated or upset, (b) fairly gracefully adapt.
42. I am usually more: (a) speculative than realistic, (b) realistic than speculative.
43. Concerning the future, I am more comfortable with: (a) careful plans in place, (b) an attitude of going with the flow.
44. Living life with a sense of anticipation and of the approaching future is: (a) a good description of me, (b) not particularly true of me because I tend to live in an ever present now.
45. I am often seen by others as: (a) lacking enthusiasm or as being detached, (b) enthused and involved.
46. In my opinion it is worse to: (a) be in a rut, (b) have your head in the clouds.
47. I prefer experiences that awaken emotions: (a) only if they have positive emotion, or little or no risk of negative emotion, (b) any emotion (positive or negative) rather than experiences with no emotional content.
48. I am known to people primarily for: (a) my ideas, my visions, the possibilities I propose, (b) my actions, what I have actually done.
49. I tend to be drawn more toward efforts to: (a) convince the "head" of others, (b) touch the "heart" of others.
50. I am more attracted to: (a) imaginative people, (b) sensible people.

69

51. Interpersonal relationships in my life are: (a) important, but not more important than some other aspects of my life, (b) clearly what is most important in my life.
52. I am more likely to trust my: (a) hunches, (b) experiences.
53. In judging or evaluating a situation I am more swayed by: (a) rules or principles than circumstances, (b) circumstances than rules or principles.
54. I generally view common sense as: (a) frequently questionable, (b) rarely questionable.

(Some items adapted from Gray-Wheelwright and from Keirsey Temperament Sorter)

Jungian Personality Inventory
Answer Sheet

	a	?	b
1	2		
5	1		
9		0	
13			1
17			2

Example:

choice "a" is very true of me

choice "a" is somewhat true of me

cannot decide OR right in the middle

choice "b" is somewhat true of me

choice "b" is very true of me

	a	?	b
1			
5			
9			
13			
17			
21			
25			
29			
33			
37			
41			
45			
49			
53			

	a	?	b
2			
6			
10			
14			
18			
22			
26			
30			
34			
38			
42			
46			
50			
54			

	a	?	b
3			
7			
11			
15			
19			
23			
27			
31			
35			
39			
43			
47			
51			

	a	?	b
4			
8			
12			
16			
20			
24			
28			
32			
36			
40			
44			
48			
52			

$\bigcirc$T2 $\bigcirc$F2 $\bigcirc$I2 $\bigcirc$S2

$\bigcirc$T1 $\bigcirc$F1 $\bigcirc$I1 $\bigcirc$S1

____ (T1) + ____ (T2) = ____   ____ (I1) + ____ (I2) = ____

____ (F1) + ____ (F2) = ____   ____ (S1) + ____ (S2) = ____

Having completed the inventory, you are now ready to tabulate your results. Your calculations will produce scores on four scales, one for each of the four functions of the psyche as described by Jung.

Work first with the vertical column on the extreme left-hand side of the answer sheet. Add up the points you have assigned to choice "a" for items 1, 5, 9, 13, 17, etc. Write this sum in the circle labeled T1. Then work with the vertical column of answers where you gave points to choice "b" for items 1, 5, 9, 13, 17, etc. Write this sum in the circle labeled F1. Proceed in the same fashion in order to get sums you can write in each labeled circle (i.e., I1, S1, T2, etc.). Finally add your T1 and T2 scores to get your overall score on the "thinking" function. Add your F1 and F2 scores for your score on "feeling"; I1 and I2, for "intuition"; and, S1 and S2, for "sensation."

Of course, a description is needed for each of these functions. The connotations you have for words like "thinking" or "intuition" may not be what Jung intended. The key to the meaning of these scale scores is the notion of polarities. In Jung's sytem of thought about the personality, the human psyche is best understood in terms of internal dualities, polar tensions. For example, we might think of gender as a polarity. Most types of metaphysical teaching agree that the human soul is neither exclusively masculine nor feminine. It is, instead, both. There is an archetypal feminine component or "yin" and an archetypal masculine component or "yang." In a particular incarnation, a soul manifests one side of the polarity over the other, but even the unmanifest pole is still a part of the individual's being. Jung labeled the unconscious feminine pole of a man the "anima" and the unconscious masculine pole of a woman the "animus."

However, for Jung, gender is not one of the key polarities for understanding human temperament. Instead, he identifies two principal polar tensions, which give us the four functions. The first of these concerns how you make evaluations in daily life circumstances. Jung felt that there were two primary ways in which evaluations or judgments could be made, and they were mutually exclusive (i.e., when you are doing it one way, you cannot be doing it the other way simultaneously).

The first mode of evaluation is what Jung called "thinking." By this he meant the logical, analytic process which measures a situation by rules, laws, principles or standards. There is an objectivity and consistency in the process used by "thinking types" as they arrive at their evaluation. The polar opposite is what Jung called "feeling." This involves evaluations which are more subjective and are based on personal values rather than the more external laws or criteria of the "thinking" function. The "feeling type" judges or evaluates based upon the uniqueness of each circumstance. Things are more situational. Memories and feelings which the circumstance evokes are influential.

Half of the items on the inventory were based on this first polar tension. You can look back at your answer sheet to see which questions concerned this thinking/feeling polarity. For those 27 items, points which you gave to "a" choices went toward your thinking score; points to "b" choices went toward your feeling score. Keep in mind, no matter what your results may be, that *both* poles are within you. The question is rather which of the two is most featured by your temperament. If you scored high on thinking, it does not mean that you are a callous person who never feels anything. Rather, it implies that you are more comfortable with or inclined toward objective, logical evaluations. If you scored high on feeling it does not mean that you are a feather-brained person who can never think straight. Instead, it indicates a preference in style for how you meet and measure life.

What if your score is balanced, virtually the same for both poles. This kind of result could have at least three possible meanings. First is the possibility that this inventory did not ask quite the right questions to draw out of you a proper reading of your temperament on this polarity. Perhaps from the description of the poles you get a sense for which one you feature more often, even if the inventory results are inconclusive. Another possibility, however, is that this is a transition time in your life, a period where you are shifting from one pole to the other. The apparent "balance" is actually indicative of change, like catching a glimpse of you on top of a fence as you climb from one field to the adjoining one. Such transitions in temperament may happen occasionally, but they are not frequent in one's life. Many people go through their entire lives and maintain a single temperament style.

The third possibility is that this polarity is rather balanced because these two functions are what Jung called "auxiliary functions," and the distinctiveness of your temperament style is not created by this polarity but instead by a clear difference in the other polarity (i.e., sensation/intuition). For example, you might have scored significantly higher on sensation than intuition, and at the same time have scores on thinking and feeling that are numerically similar. In Jungian terminology your "primary function" would be sensation (that is, sensation is the primary descriptive term of your temperament). Your "inferior function" would be intuition ("inferior" not in the sense of "bad" but instead as "unconscious"). And your "auxiliary functions" would be thinking and feeling. Some readers will find that the results of their inventory fit this model; others will find that each of the two polarities yields a distinctly predominant function.

The question of balance is also important here. It does not appear from his writings that Jung felt the ideal would be function scores on the inventory that were identical. In other words, the individuation process or the living of your soul's mission can be accomplished even if you are strongly a certain temperament type. A problem arises, however, if you are alienated from one of the psychological functions and unable to call upon it when it is needed and appropriate. The ideal, therefore, might be clear access to all the functions and familiarity with them, even though in daily living one or two of them are especially prominent in your personality.

These ideas about the thinking/feeling polarity also hold true for the second polarity which Jung felt was central to the make-up of the personality. This one concerns how you make perceptions in life. The first mode of perception is what Jung called "sensation." This pole entails the use of the physical senses to perceive life. It is exclusively concerned with what is "here and now" as concrete physical reality. When you perceive life with this function, you deal with life in a very present-oriented kind of practicality. Its polar opposite is what Jung called "intuition," not merely psychic perception, but more broadly the use of creative imagination to perceive the possibilities of life. Intuition, in this sense, is future-oriented; it can perceive what is coming or what might be, but that which is not yet manifest in a physical way.

Half of the items on the inventory concerned the sensation/intuition polarity. Take note of the items which contributed to your "I" or "S" scores by referring to your answer sheet. On those items the points you assigned to the "a" choices corresponded to the intuition scale and those to the "b" choice corresponded to the sensation scale. Keep in mind, once again, that both poles are within you, but that your personality likely features one mode of perception over the other. The comments regarding "balance" on the thinking/feeling polarity are also relevant to this other polarity.

To further clarify the meaning of each of the four functions, try to apply these insights by John Welch in his fine book on Jungian individuation called *Spiritual Pilgrims:*

"Sensation and intuition. . .have to do with the way whereby we perceive our experiences. A person with a highly developed sensation function perceives experience through the sense organs as well as through interior sensations. This function is sometimes called the reality function since it is alert to factual detail. It tells us that something exists.

"The intuition function, on the other hand, operates almost as a 'sixth sense.' This function perceives almost instinctively . . . Perceptions are mediated to the intuitive function in an unconscious way. It is not as alert to the sense data, but it perceives the meaning and possibility of a situation.

"Thinking and feeling. . .determine the manner whereby we judge, or come to conclusions about, our perceptions. The thinking function uses a logical process that links ideas together which then lead to a conclusion. It is an intellectual function which seeks to understand something. The feeling function uses a process of evaluation leading to like or dislike, acceptance or rejection. Something is accepted or rejected depending upon whether it arouses a pleasant or unpleasant feeling."

Relating the Functions to Your Soul's Mission

We have stressed how important it is to understand the personality and its habitual ways of functioning. The discovery and living of your soul's purpose rests largely upon being able to free yourself from your personality's mechanical, automatic habits. This is not to say that once you have found your mission in life you will cease to have a personality. Nor is it to say that you must radically alter your personality temperament in order to live your soul's purpose.

Instead, the problem that you and every seeker faces can be summarized in this fashion. Your personality has certain strong predispositions for perceiving and evaluating life. There is nothing inherently wrong with your personality type. Your soul's mission can be lived with those predominant functions. However, making heavy use of those predominant functions, you have slipped into habitual ways of seeing and reacting to life, you have gotten hypnotized into a sleeplike existence of routine. This may have worked very well to produce a comfortable, predictable life, but it probably does not result in a creative, dynamic life experience that will be fulfilling.

The antidote is two-fold. First, by exercises in self-observation you can slowly redeem those predominant functions from unconscious habit to wakeful creativity. Second, you can periodically make efforts to engage the weaker functions. This second approach is based upon one of the most significant insights in all of Jung's work: the inferior function(s) is closely connected with the deeper levels of the soul.

Consider the model of the mind which we have seen in Jung's psychology. Like an iceberg, only a small portion of the human mind extends into wakeful consciousness. Usually "hidden" from view are the regions of the unconscious, the personal unconscious and the collective unconscious. If we examine one of the principal polarities of the psyche and place it on the model, it would look like the diagram below. In this example, we see depicted a person who has scored higher on the thinking function than on the feeling function.

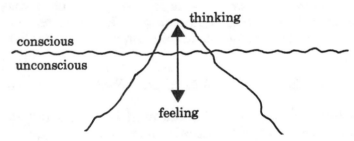

In other words, to say that you are a thinking type means that you have integrated this function into your conscious life, the way you go about evaluating most of your daily life experiences. But in this example, what has become of your feeling function? The notion of polarities presupposes that you have a feeling function within you. The answer is that it is "embedded" in your unconscious life.

This principle leads to the conclusion that something quite remarkable happens when such an "embedded" function surfaces. It brings with it impressions from deep within the soul. It is tainted with the content of the personal unconscious, or sometimes the collective unconscious. As it surfaces into conscious life, such an "inferior function" can be a vehicle for messages, insights, and knowledge from deep within yourself. Certainly not everything that it brings with it will be a profound revelation about your soul's mission. You will have to use discrimination. However, you can gain important clues about the ideal of your soul and its intentions for this lifetime. This can happen as you systematically make the effort to bring into conscious life the functions which your psychological type (or temperament) rarely uses.

Consider our first example: a person whose temperament makes frequent use of the thinking function and whose feeling function is usually not called forth into conscious life. Suppose this individual periodically puts herself into a situation where the thinking function is not appropriate. It might be for only an hour or two a week. The activity might be something like a sculpture workshop or a dance class—something that lends itself to subjective feelings instead of logical analysis. What can happen to her during those moments?

First, we should keep in mind that the point of such a selective discipline is not to turn her from a thinking type into a feeling type. Instead, the point is to give her a chance to experience herself in a different way. She is making a specific effort to engage life from a perspective that is not her normal or habitual one. In so doing she is likely to feel some awkwardness and she is likely to feel her more familiar dominant function trying to regain control (i.e., to analytically figure out how to make something in the clay, or to logically control her dance steps). But soon she will find that a different function serves her best in this situation. And by inviting to the surface this often forgotten feeling function she opens herself to a different way of experiencing.

During such moments she may suddenly experience her sense of identity as something that is off of her mechanical personality wheel. Or she may get unexpected impressions or insights coming from deep within her soul. They are most likely unrelated to the actual sculpting or dancing, but speak to the broader question of what her life is really about or what the next step should be in living her mission. It is not that her soul's purpose is to become a dancer or a sculptor, but rather that these exercises she has chosen to do provide opportunities for inspiration and new ways of seeing life emerge. Such "moments" are difficult to describe, but anyone who has experienced them knows how significant they can be. The

Jungian model of the mind and the four functions help us to see how the process can work.

Let us think as well about the other examples which are possible. Suppose there is a man who is the mirror image of the woman in the previous example—his feeling function is well integrated into conscious life, but the thinking function is embedded in the unconscious. What kind of periodic activity might he add to his life style as a discipline in awakening the unused function? There are many activities that direct one toward the use of analytical methods for making evaluations. Perhaps he would enroll in a philosophy course for one evening a week. It would be an exercise in which his logical abilities would need to come to the surface. Not only would this serve the purpose of making him a "more well-rounded person" it might also give him moments of experiencing himself in a different way.

Let us suppose that he has to struggle with the course just to get a passing grade—clearly it is not his soul's purpose to be a philosopher—and yet something special may occasionally happen to him in those classes. There may be moments in which he sees and relates to life in a novel way, compared to the habitual ways of his personality. There may be experiences in which a deep level of his soul is revealed. As the thinking function comes forth from within him it may bring with it an insight or universal law that is especially significant for him at this point in his life, something his more familiar feeling function was unlikely to have provided.

The same sort of process is relevant to the sensation/intuition polarity. Imagine a woman whose personality more readily features the sensation function. It might even be the same woman who favored thinking over feeling. How could she engage her intuition function from time to time? What kind of consciously chosen activity would be likely to put her familiar sensation function "on hold" temporarily and allow the intuition function to emerge? It might be something that would use her imagination or get her to consider the possibilities in things. For example, she might get involved in music reverie workshops or classes. Guided imagery experiences can be a valuable source of direction from the soul for any person, no matter what type function. But they can be especially significant for the person whose intuition function has been embedded in the unconscious life of the soul.

Or, suppose there is a man who is well grounded in his

conscious life use of the intuition function, but rarely engages his sensation function. What kind of periodic activities could stimulate this same process for him? Anything that pushes him to deal with physical reality in the here and now is a good candidate. For example, some intuitive types have had important experiences by getting more in touch with the physical body and working with it in a pragmatic way. This individual might choose to take a training course in massage. The practical, physical realities involved in occasionally giving a massage to someone else could be the very activity that would give him those "moments" of deeper insight or understanding. Again, the practice of giving massages may be quite incidental to his actual life's mission. But this discipline could be the source of inspiration or even freeing encounters with a deep level of himself from which his actual mission does spring.

Take time now and think about this sort of discipline for yourself. Think of it as an experiment. The two or three activities you choose will be things to occasionally include in your life style, hopefully in a regular way. You can use the worksheet/chart on the following page as a place to write down your thoughts. Quite likely some or all of the activities you choose will have an awkward or foreign flavor to them, simply because your habitual personality is not accustomed to meeting life in this fashion. Certainly you cannot expect that every time you complete these activities you will have some profound insight into your soul's mission. But in a simple and quiet way, these experiences will be nudging you toward a sense of personal identity from which your soul's purpose can be seen and lived.

Jungian Functions
Getting in Touch with Embedded Inferior Functions

Scored high on	Embedded function	Sample activities	My experiments
T	F	using the arts to awaken subjective impressions; deepening relationships; getting in touch with memories	
F	T	using logic and analysis; planning; making objective evaluations instead of personal opinions	
I	S	fixing things; developing mechanical aptitudes; getting in touch with the physical body, being practical or pragmatic; punctual	
S	I	dream study; music and imagination; looking for possibilities; setting ideals, trusting hunches	

Chapter Four
FIVE STEPS TO DISCOVERING
YOUR SOUL'S PURPOSE

We are now at the point of synthesis. The principles and concepts from the Cayce readings, Gurdjieff's system, and Jung's psychology can be blended into a comprehensive model for finding one's mission in life. These complementary approaches provide the seeker with practical steps for discovering the destiny of the soul, that ideal which the soul intended upon incarnation.

A starting point for this synthesis is a review and then expansion of one idea which has already been discussed. A new "center of identity" is possible for you, a way of knowing yourself and your life that is "off the wheel" of your personality. This different sense of personal identity is related to the individuality/essence/Self as it has been previously defined. Perhaps it is unlikely that you would be able to be constantly in that new sense of identity, but you can learn to know it so well that you can return to it at will. You can so fully discover that your real identity is this new center, that your personality becomes more and more "passive."

In this case the word "passive" does not necessarily mean that your persona or appearance to others suddenly becomes one of timidity or meekness. Instead, it connotes that the personality (no matter what its characteristics) no longer has such a tight, controlling grip on your feelings of identity. As the personality becomes more passive, you find it easier and easier to separate from it in consciousness and to know yourself as individuality/essence/Self.

There are two primary ways in which this work is done. The awakening of a center of identity from the personality wheel can be aided by your own efforts. For example, the practice of meditation or the use of self-observation techniques stimulates this shift in awareness. Exercises to awaken and train the will are also helpful. Your personality wheel is largely will-less (or characterized by a "sleeping" will). Your individuality center, as we have seen in Chapter One, is fundamentally related to the will and to the ideal which you as a soul held upon coming into the earth.

But the awakening of this new center of identity can also be accomplished through another type of work—something which does not directly involve your efforts, except by making a proper response. There are constructive influences which come to you which arise from beyond yourself. These influences are, in a sense, from beyond material life. They may manifest as physical events, yet their point of origin is not to be explained in terms of physical causality.

In the language of the Cayce readings, there is offered to you "For *today* [and for every day!]. . .the *opportunity* to make manifest that which *is* ideal. . ." (816-10) In other words, each day the universal forces draw into the sphere of your life certain people, circumstances and situations. These special opportunities are each a challenge. With each you have the chance to get off your personality wheel and respond to the opportunity from your individuality center. Each day the loving, wise forces of the universe place in your life path certain situations which hold a key for you. If they are met properly, they are a movement back toward the path of your soul's purpose.

In Jung's system of thought, these kinds of influences are mentioned in two ways. First is the notion that within your unconscious there is an impetus toward wholeness. This impetus cannot be explained in terms of material laws and yet it can be observed, both in your inner life (e.g., dreams) and in outer events. The second way concerns these events. Circumstances which appear to have an inexplicable degree of coincidence were described by Jung as the Law of Synchronicity.

Put poetically, we might say that "synchronicity is the answer to your question trying to find itself." That is to say, any important question you pose—such as "what is my purpose for this lifetime?"—has an answer. However, that answer has remained unconscious and seeks to come to consciousness, to "find itself." The solution to your question tries to make itself conscious through your experience, and synchronistic occurrences are a primary way in which that can be accomplished.

In essence this law states that situations in life which seem to be random and arbitrary can be directed by an ordering principle which is not based on physical laws of cause and effect. In other words, there are types of connectedness in the universe which are not reducible to linear time and physical energy. This law produces influences in our lives, and those influences often create situations which appear as "meaningful coincidences."

Suppose, for example, that you get up in the morning and at breakfast overhear your two teenagers talking about racing cars. That in itself is not significant. Perhaps you have never heard them talk about this topic, but it is certainly a theme that young people might be interested in. At the time, you think nothing of it. However, later that day, sitting in a waiting room at the dentist, you absent-mindedly pick up a magazine and randomly open it. To your surprise you have opened to a feature story about a race car driver. You probably note the unusualness of this minor coincidence. Then at the office that afternoon, your boss comes into the office, excited to tell you about the sports car he has decided to buy, one which he intends to use occasionally for racing.

With this third occurrence the coincidence of events seems too uncanny to pass off merely as chance. It is clear that these three events did not physically cause each other. Your teenage sons did not call your boss and tell him to talk to you about his race car purchase. Your boss did not talk to the dentist and ask that this particular magazine be placed near the chair where you would be waiting. If the events are linked, it is in a non-causal fashion.

For Jung this might be an example of synchronicity, a meaningful coincidence. But what *is* the meaning of these events? In some cases, it is the content of the coincidences that imparts a meaning. In this way, synchronicity can serve as a type of guidance. In our example, the meaning of these coincidences could be guidance to take more of an interest in racing cars (literally or symbolically). On the other hand, there is a second type of meaning found in synchronistic occurrences. It relates to the state of awareness into which one is propelled in that moment of recognizing that the unusual coincidences have happened. There is a moment which may last for three seconds or several hours in which you can feel a mystery of life. It is a state of awareness in which you know that the universe includes forces and influences which are beyond mechanistic, material laws. You may experience this as a bodily sensation. It might be a tingling in your spine which accompanies the thought that something is helping to direct and order your life. Or you may experience it as a feeling of awe.

Take a moment and think about your own life. Can you recall synchronistic occurrences? Were there some which seemed to have a guidance quality in their content? Were there others that instead served to shift your feelings about life, that reminded you that forces bigger than yourself (even bigger than material laws) were involved in shaping your experiences? You shall soon see how these kinds of synchronistic events can be helpful influences for shifting your sense of personal identity from the personality wheel to the individuality center.

In Gurdjieff's system there is a clear distinction made among types of influences. First, there are those which arise from material life. These influences are governed by laws of physical causation and even, we might add, karmic causation. However, there are other influences which can potentially shape your experiences in life. These have their origin outside of physical life, although they may manifest in terms of material life occurrences.

We might even speculate that there is a conceptual overlap between Jung's notion of synchronicity and Gurdjieff's idea of types of influences. Although the concepts are not identical, we might consider that synchronistic events are somehow directed by this second category of influences. The parallel seems even more striking if we broaden the notion of synchronicity to include the occurrence of circumstances and events in life which coincide with inner needs for growth. Recall the hypothesis from the Cayce readings that each day life will place before you opportunities which relate to your soul's ideal and its mission. Could these opportunities be seen somewhat like synchronistic events? Could these occurrences be viewed as the product of Gurdjieff's second category of influences—influences that have their origin outside of material life?

These ideas can be depicted in the model below. Here we can organize the concepts of the personality wheel, psychological functions and types of influence into a single diagram.

Material
Life
Influences

Influences
Arising from
Beyond Material Life

The oval in its entirety corresponds to your being, the totality of your soul. One aspect of your being is your personality, depicted as a wheel which revolves around a chief feature or chief misunderstanding. The personality itself is made up of many subpersonalities or many "I"s. Each "I" claims to be the totality of your being when it is "on stage," when it has the focus of your attention and is the source of your sense of identity. Each "I" has associated with it a set of habitual traits which are depicted as spokes of the wheel.

In the course of a typical day, the wheel is "bumped" many times by influences which arise from material life. Influences of this first category serve to keep the wheel of your personality turning, apparently creating movement but in reality serving only to bring you back to the same places. These "bumps" also shift your sense of personal identity from one subpersonality "I" to another. As material life gives you unexpected "shocks," it is virtually impossible for your personality to maintain a consistent feeling of identity. Lacking a consistent "I" you are unable to really follow through on a plan or a vision, and the living of your soul's mission is not within your reach.

Influences flow into your being through the psychological functions. Your temperament is such that some of the functions are better integrated into your conscious, physical life. Because of this orientation, the influences arising from material life (i.e., Gurdjieff's first type of influence) most readily flow in to you through those well-used functions. The functions are like doorways into your being.

For example, suppose that on the Jungian temperament inventory you scored higher on thinking than on feeling, and higher on intuition than on sensation. Thinking and intuition are well integrated into your "normal" way of responding to life. We could say that your personality wheel is most often kept active by "bumps" from material life which flow through the doorway (the psychological functions) of thinking and intuition. Your personality habits are *especially* kept active by your logical, analytical evaluations and your imaginative perception of what the future could offer. Your ways of analytically evaluating things tend to perpetuate your personality; your imaginative notions of the future are usually just an extension of your personality and its sense of identity.

What, then, of your relatively unused functions? In this example, what has become of the functions of feeling and sensation? Occasionally, they may serve as doorways to the influences which arise from material life—that is, the influences which keep your personality wheel turning. However, as depicted in the model above, those functions are more readily available for influences whose origin is beyond material life, influences not directly related to the concerns of the personality wheel. In this example, the functions of feeling and sensation are playing a role whereby influences of this second category can touch the individual.

As you consider this example, you may ask yourself how a function as pragmatic and physically oriented as "sensation" could be a doorway for influences from *beyond* material life. Certainly, it is true that the sensation function deals with things which can be physically perceived. But keep in mind that the second category of influences has its *origin* beyond material-life laws of causation. The Jungian examples of synchronicity take on a physical form, even though the ordering principle directing the occurrences may not be governed by material laws of cause and effect. With this in mind, we can see how even the sensation function could serve as a doorway for the second type of influences.

One of the primary problems we face is also depicted in this model. Influences from beyond material life usually are not attended to. Even though you have psychological functions which are particularly suited to the task, their input is most often ignored or resisted. You tend to focus attention upon your identity as personality, while the second type of influences do little or no work in shaping a new sense of identity and life's mission for you.

However, another possibility exists. In a second version of the model, depicted below, influences of the second type *are* attended to. Those influences serve the purpose of shaping and strengthening the individuality or essence center within you. Through an act of will you can direct your attention toward the impact of these influences. In some cases, these influences act in an inner way to produce feelings, impressions and insights which take your sense of personal identity off the personality wheel and toward the individuality center. In other cases, those influences manifest as physical events and opportunities which give you a special chance to respond from your individuality instead of your personality.

The individuality center is strengthened by your frequent movement to its sense of identity. Each time you "remember yourself" (in the language of Gurdjieff's system) you make it easier and more likely that in the future you shall do so again.

A *Five-Step Process*

Let us suppose that you have begun an on-going work to understand your personality wheel and its frequent control of your thinking, feeling and acting. Through disciplines, such as dream study and self-observation exercises, you will continue to gain important insights into the habitual, mechanical parts of yourself, the parts that often frustrate any creative movement in the direction of your real mission. Let us also suppose that you are making efforts from "your end" to get in touch with your individuality center. You keep a regular meditation time, you work on exercises to awaken and develop your will, and you carefully watch for influences of the second category in your inner and outer life. In addition to this on-going preparatory work, you can also initiate a more structured, systematic search to discover your soul's purpose.

Step #1: Give a tentative label to your individuality/essence/ Self identity with a "spiritual ideal." This foundation-building step is crucial if the following steps are to be successful. The formulation of a clear statement of your mission in life rests upon genuine understanding of your ideal.

Perhaps no topic is more central to the philosophy found in the Cayce readings. In virtually every area of Cayce's work, this subject emerges in a key way. In the physical readings it is found. We might see these readings as precursors of the modern holistic health movement; and in a fashion that is often left out of current "holistic" approaches, the Cayce health readings emphasized the role of ideals in the healing process. For example, the patient must have a sense of why he or she wants to get well. Without such a sense of ideal or purpose, the physical symptoms may be removed with medication or surgery without a real healing in consciousness. Without an ideal, the "healing" may be only temporary and a new set of symptoms is likely to manifest.

Ideals are also a significant aspect of Cayce's approach to dream interpretation. The very technique of deciphering a dream can be viewed as measuring the content of the dream experience against the dreamer's ideals. [Editor's note: See Dr. Thurston's book *How to Interpret Your Dreams* in which an entire chapter is devoted to the details of how ideals can be used as an interpretive technique.] In Cayce's readings on how to pray and meditate, ideals play a central role. The affirmation, upon which the meditator seeks to place all conscious attention, is a brief, verbal expression of the spiritual ideal. In the readings which describe the processes of reincarnation and karma, ideals are a significant influence. Karmic influences themselves grow out of the ideals which have been held in various lifetimes (some of those ideals having been more constructive than others).

What is meant by your "spiritual ideal"? Is it something unconscious, something known only to your soul? Is it that sense of ideal and purpose that your soul intended upon incarnating? Earlier in this book the word "ideal" has been used in that way. But in this first step of our five-step process, we want to focus on the *conscious* component of ideals. In other words, what is the best conscious understanding that you currently have of this deep sense of ideal which is held by your soul for this lifetime? Or, put more exactly, what label can you put on that sense of personal identity from which your purpose shall be lived? Who is this Self that Cayce calls your individuality? Have you caught a glimpse or two of yourself as this identity? Have you had special moments in which you knew yourself in a different way?

The word or phrase you will soon choose to represent your spiritual ideal is both a statement of aspiration and a reminder of something you have experienced, however briefly. It is aspiration because the spiritual ideal calls you to be the Self you rarely remember to be. It is the recollection of personal experience because, without having had at least a fleeting taste of that different identity, the spiritual ideal will remain a dry, theoretical concept in your life.

The notion of your spiritual ideal rooted in an actual, personal experience cannot be stressed too much. It is also fine to have hopes related to things beyond the scope of personal experience. You may trust the words of others more advanced along the spiritual path than you are and have faith that someday you will have similar experiences. No doubt, this kind of aspiration and hope is a powerful influence for spiritual growth. But the spiritual ideal is best understood as something different than this kind of faith.

Something special takes place when you consciously identify an experience or experiences from your past which have had a spiritually quickening effect upon you. When you choose a spiritual ideal which is related to a taste or glimpse that you have actually received of your individuality/essence/Self center, then there is no room for doubt about its reality. Admittedly, you may have questions about your capacity to sustain that sense of personal identity, but it is not a matter of doubting that that place in consciousness exists. Because you know so clearly and so personally that this spiritual ideal has reality, you can at any moment use your will to call it back to mind, *unfettered by doubt about its reality.*

A spiritual ideal which is rooted in a personal experience also allows you to avoid another pitfall in setting ideals. If you are like most others, there is a tendency to set your spiritual ideal in terms of "shoulds" and "oughts" of key authority figures in your life, even spiritual authority figures. Something deeper within your soul, however, will not feel comfortable with this. It will rebel if your spiritual ideal is set in terms of what your parents or schoolteachers or church leaders have said your ideals ought to be. Actually it is a shortcut of your own personality wheel to set a spiritual ideal in such a manner. Remember that your personality wheel is largely the product of what you have taken on from others. Your personality will tend to suggest a spiritual ideal made up of such "shoulds" and "oughts" which come from others. In fact, to allow your life to be guided by a spiritual ideal which has been determined that way serves only to perpetuate the control of that wheel. This gives a new meaning to "reinventing the wheel."

Instead, your spiritual ideal is best set as a sense of personal identity that is uniquely you. Beyond habit and routine, it describes a place of clarity from which you are free to create and live your mission. A spiritual ideal, in the fullness of its potential for power, may have a visionary/revelatory quality to it. In other words, it is based on an experience of yourself, however brief or long ago, in which was revealed to you a vision of who you really are. For some people the vision was vague and fuzzy, but different enough from the typical way of knowing oneself that there was obviously something special about it. For other people, the revelation was extraordinarily distinct and overwhelming in its impact.

Such a "vision" or "revelation" has not come for most people as an ethereal, hallucinogenic experience. More often these moments have come in a quieter way in the midst of daily living. But they are always received with an element of surprise. There is an unexpectedness to their quality. In fact, they often leave your personality self feeling uncomfortable, because your individuality self usually sees life in a quite different way.

Can you recall one or more such moments in your life? Are there key experiences from your past that are still profoundly influential in your spiritual quest? Are there times when you tasted or caught a glimpse of another way of knowing yourself? Those experiences are highly significant in the task of this first of five steps. Drawing largely upon those important memories, set a spiritual ideal for your life. Give your individuality/ essence/Self identity a label by which it can be known. Don't be concerned if your word or phrase does not sound lofty enough. What matters first of all is that the words you choose make sense to you. What matters further is that your spiritual ideal be real enough to you that there is no room to doubt its reality, even if you do feel lacking in capacity to be that identity when you want to.

Your spiritual ideal is likely to change as you progress in the discovery process. That is to say, your understanding of the best label for your individuality center will probably change. It is not a matter of the ideal of your soul for this lifetime changing, but rather your vision of what that intentionality encompasses will become clearer.

Let's consider two examples of this five-stage process of finding one's mission in life. The two individuals we will consider spent several months of careful self-study and application in order to arrive at a preliminary understanding of the purpose of the soul for this lifetime. As we proceed with a description of each of the five steps, we will examine how these two people accomplished a particular step.

Robert was a 37-year-old businessman. By all outward appearances he was the model of the successful man. He was founder and president of a small business that employed about forty people. He was father of three children and had a marriage that seemed to be going reasonably well. Yet despite many enviable accomplishments in material life he felt unfulfilled. Something was still missing in his life. Robert felt

Soul's Purpose Diagram

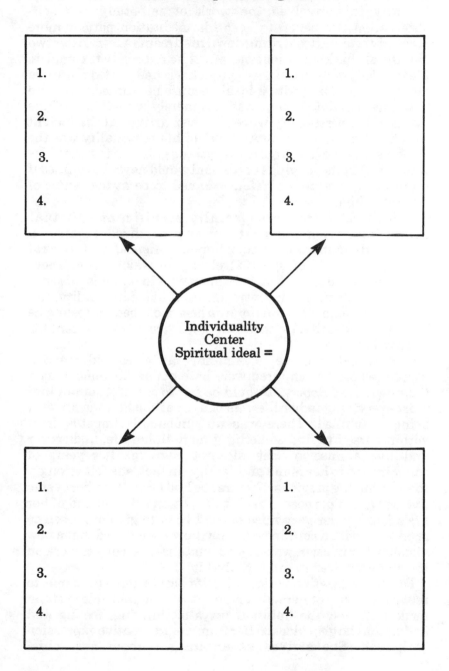

that he had not yet found what he was born to do.

He entered into a commitment to find his mission in life. Initially this involved the work of self-study and self-observation. He began to keep his meditation periods more regularly and started writing down his dreams again. After two months of this kind of renewed effort he felt ready to complete the first step of the five-step approach. He had waited these two months to set his spiritual ideal because he wanted to be sure that this foundation step was not merely a restating of the ideals of his personality wheel. He had arrived at the insight that the "chief misunderstanding" of his personality was the compulsion to be in charge of everything going on in his life. He was sure that the longings of his soul would never be fulfilled if such a consciousness of life continued to be at the center of living for him.

Robert reflected on especially significant spiritual experiences from his past, on two or three dreams, a particularly important meditation experience, and several striking moments of spiritual clarity in waking life. These experiences had given him brief moments in an unusual sense of personal identity. They were a taste of his individuality, and he chose a single word that for him best described the feeling he had in that identity. He chose the word "trust" to represent his spiritual ideal.

Our second example is Amanda, a 54-year-old married woman whose two children were both out of the home and on their own. Like Robert, it would be fair to say of Amanda that most everything in her life was okay. Yet she had the sense of being unfulfilled. There was an undeniable impetus from within herself to find something more in her life, to discover and live a mission. She did not begrudge her years of commitment to her home and family. In fact, she felt strongly that during the previous 27 years she had been doing her best to live her soul's purpose. She felt that during that period of her life's journey her very mission had been to give of herself to family life with a certain spirit. But now she realized that a new vision of her mission was needed, and she was ready to work on the steps required in order to find it.

During a lengthy period of self-observation she came to recognize many of her subpersonalities. She was able to stand aside and view the habitual ways of thinking, feeling and acting that largely blocked her from a more creative expression of herself. She arrived at an insight about her "chief misunderstanding," the hub of her personality wheel. It was best described with the words, "I don't deserve anything better." Her various subpersonalities all revolved around this limiting notion. Her habitual, mechanical ways of being in the world all seemed to grow out of this idea. Even some of her greatest talents and strengths were caught up in this stifling concept that she was not deserving.

Like Robert, she drew upon the memories of actual life experiences to formulate her spiritual ideal. These special moments in her past had given her a glimpse of a different sense of personal identity, something quite different than her personality wheel. To describe her individuality center, she chose the words "oneness of all life."

Now is the time for *you* to set your own spiritual ideal, to give a descriptive label to your own individuality center as you have experienced it, however briefly. What word or phrase is appropriate for you? In addition to the examples of Robert and Amanda, here are phrases that others have come up with in completing this first step: joyful creativity, peaceful centeredness that takes life one moment at a time, loving freedom, serenity, and servant of God. However, these phrases are merely samples. What is important is that you pick words that are personally meaningful.

You can record the words you chose in the center circle of your "soul's purpose diagram" found on page 91. That circle represents your individuality center; and by writing your spiritual ideal in it, you are labeling this place in consciousness from which Steps 2 through 5 will proceed.

Step #2: Reconstellate your soul's talents around the individuality center. Once you have gotten a clear enough image of your individuality identity to give it a label, you can consider the tools of expression available to it. With Step #2 you are not yet specifying ways in which you, as individuality, would express yourself in the world. That will come in Step #3. Instead, at this stage you will identify the key strengths, abilities, skills and aptitudes with which your individuality center can work to live its mission.

Up until now most of those talents of your soul have either been latent and unexpressed, or they have been incorporated into your personality wheel. As a part of that wheel, many of your talents have not only been lived automatically, unconsciously and habitually; they have also been subservient to the hub of your wheel: the chief misunderstanding. These strengths and abilities have tended to constellate themselves around a fundamentally erroneous way of seeing life. They have arranged themselves in an orderly, structured pattern which served just one purpose: to maintain the control of personality.

When your talents and strengths are wrapped up in your personality wheel, they are usually experienced in one of two ways. First, they may appear as clearly recognizable talents, but ones which do not produce for you a sense of fulfillment in life. For example, Robert had a talent for being organized. It had become one of the principal spokes of his wheel. His friends and he himself knew that he had this strength within his being. Yet that talent had been used to serve his chief misunderstanding: to compulsively try to be in charge of everything in his life. As a personality, he used the considerable skill of an organizer to maintain control: of his company, of his family life, of his time. He even tried to keep his spiritual life organized and assert some measure of control over his relationship to God. But the result was that he was not fulfilled in life. This talent of his soul was being wasted; it was not leading him any closer to his soul's mission.

There is a second way in which you can experience one of your talents when it is wrapped up in your personality wheel. Its subservience to the chief misunderstanding can distort it so that it comes out looking like a fault or weakness. For example, another of the spokes on Robert's wheel was his automatic, mechanical tendency to be a manipulator. Yet that weakness of character had embedded within it a strength of his soul: to be a motivator. The problem was created by this talent being distorted by his personality's mistaken notion that it always had to stay in control of people and events. In a similar fashion, Robert had a talent within himself described as a good sense of humor. But as a spoke on the wheel rotating around and serving the chief misunderstanding, it came out looking like a fault: he would jokingly put people down to gain control of a situation.

Finally, you should also realize that some of the talents of your soul have not yet come to your awareness because you have been so identified with your personality identity. Suppose, for example, that a strength of your soul is so contrary in nature to your chief misunderstanding that it is even unlikely that the hub of your wheel could find a way of distorting it to its own ends. Such a talent will not likely have shown up on the inventory you completed earlier. You don't know about it yet. However, as you more and more frequently have experiences in which you know yourself as individuality instead of personality, the recognition of that talent will come. For example, Robert discovered a talent of his soul to be gentle, but it came only after he was well along in his work to discover and live his mission in life. As long as he had so fully identified himself with his personality wheel, it had stayed hidden. Gentleness was so contrary to being in charge of everything that it had stayed totally out of view. His chief misunderstanding had not even found a way to misuse that talent in a distorted form.

In completing Step #2 now, you will not be able to draw upon such hidden talents. As they emerge later, you may want to come back to this Step #2 and also to Step #3, and reconsider your plan in light of such newly awakened strengths. But for the time being, you will need to work with talents and strengths which you have already recognized.

On your soul's purpose diagram (see page 91) you will see that four arrows emerge from the circle in which you have labeled your individuality center. The four is arbitrary; there could just as easily have been three or five arrows in the diagram, but the number four has proven to be an easily manageable one for this exercise. Give each of the arrows a label. Identify it as one of the key strengths, abilities, aptitudes or skills of your soul. Robert labeled his four arrows with these words: motivator, organizer, harmonizer, sense of humor. Amanda labeled hers with these words: playful nature, innovative, teaching, good with plants.

Use the results of the personal inventory you have already completed (see pages 26-28). Draw upon your notes from Section 1 and Section 2(b) of the inventory. Pay particular attention to those items in Section 1 which you indicated with a double "x." Your task with Step #2 is to select four talents of your soul which might be especially needed if you are to live and express your mission in life. To a certain extent, Step #2 involves some guesswork, so label your four arrows in pencil. That will make it easier to go back and change your choices on this step if the steps which follow are not productive. This entire five-step process requires that you have such an exploratory, playful and experimenting attitude.

In selecting your four, ask yourself this question, "At an intuitive or gut level, which of my strengths are ones which I sense have a purpose to them which is well beyond how I have been using them up until now?" For some people this sense of unrealized potential is quite strong. They may not know yet the way in which a particular talent is supposed to be used, but they are very clear about which talents fit this description. When you have labeled your four arrows, you will be ready for the next step: a look at possible ways that those key talents of your soul might manifest in new ways.

Step #3: Imagine hypothetical ways that soul talents might express in life. This is a step of creative thinking, of imagining possibilities. It is to be done with a playful and experimenting perspective of your discovery process. As you work on this stage, be sure that you do not prematurely limit yourself with self-doubts which say, "Oh, I could never do that successfully!"

Other people can be helpful to you at this third step of planning and discovery. That is to say, this is the one step that does not require you to work alone. Because this is the stage of brainstorming possibilities, the ideas and suggestions of friends and fellow seekers can be invaluable. Of course, not every suggestion presented to you will strike you as one worth recording on your soul's purpose diagram. Pick those that have a "ring of truth" to you.

The principle to keep in mind for Step #3 is that, by the end of the discovery process, you will record many more possibilities than will actually prove to be a part of your soul's mission. With this step you are merely creating testable hypotheses. You will write them on the soul's purpose diagram in the rectangles which are found at the end of each arrow labeled in Step #2.

Step #3 asks you to think about this question: "If one of my key soul talents were to be lived from my individuality identity, in what ways might it express itself?" In other words, "What are the possibilities for practical manifestations of my soul's strengths, skills and aptitudes when I am living life from the identity of being individuality instead of personality?"

Those manifestations will generally fall into one of two categories. First are ways of living which involve direct service to others. Recall that this was one of the five archetypical characteristics of any soul's mission as described in the Cayce readings. The second category includes ways of living whose primary purpose or intent is "Self"-nurturing. Possibilities in this second category will be manifestations or applications of soul talents which serve to keep your identity more frequently in the individuality center.

Continuing our two examples, we will examine how Robert

and Amanda completed Step #3. After considerable brainstorming and sorting out of possibilities, Robert chose between two and four hypothetical expressions for each of the four soul talents on his diagram sheet. Every time he wrote something in one of the rectangles, he had no idea whether or not it would prove to be successful or even if it was meant to be part of his mission in life. With Step #3 all he was trying to do was create a listing of possibilities which intuitively and logically seemed to be promising.

For his arrow labeled "motivator," he arrived at three hypotheses. First was to work as a volunteer with teenagers, especially teenage boys, to help them with self-confidence and to get them motivated for adult life. He had never done this before, but it clearly fit the criterion of service to others and he sensed that he might be good at it. Second was to offer business training seminars which focus on motivating people to their best performance. Robert knew of several business education associations which sponsored such events, many of which were taught by executives like himself. Again, he had never done anything like this; but it would involve serving others with one of his talents, and he thought that perhaps this could be one piece in the overall mosaic of his soul's purpose. Third was to work as a volunteer counselor in the community, perhaps on a telephone hotline sponsored by his church. It seemed to him that a talent for motivating people might come in handy doing this kind of service.

For his arrow labeled "harmonizer," Robert selected two hypotheses to test. The first possibility involved working part time as a consultant to businesses in his community which needed help in solving communications problems. He had once brought such an expert into his company for two days and had been impressed with the results. This consultant had benefited by his role of the "objective outsider" and had been especially skillful in harmonizing the points of view of different company employees. Robert recognized in himself a similar strength to be a harmonizer and imagined that it might be fulfilling to his soul to work at least part time in such a role for other companies.

A second possibility for his strength as a harmonizer was to work in new ways within his own business organization. He imagined this as a deeper involvement in work related to the personnel department. Up until now, he had left all of those types of concerns to the manager of that department. But now he saw possibilities which might lead him to a new sense of fulfillment in his vocation. One role of the personnel department was to harmonize the abilities of employees with the tasks they were asked to do in their jobs. Sometimes this involved moving people into new positions; sometimes it involved additional training for employees to draw out of them natural talents which were not yet expressed. Robert considered the possibility of getting more involved in this kind of work on a day-to-day basis at his own company.

For his arrow labeled "organizer," he recorded four hypotheses. First was to compile ideas and to write a book. He had never tried this before, but he knew that one skill a writer might need is organizational abilities. He didn't yet know the topic on which he would try writing, but the whole idea "felt right" to him. Second was to serve as a volunteer helper at his local library during the springtime to give advice to the elderly on tax return forms. For years he had noticed that this program was offered and until now he had never considered how his talent of organizing things might be of service in this fashion.

A third possibility was to help out more at his church, perhaps in a role that involved his skill at organizing things. It occurred to him to volunteer to be church treasurer. Finally, Robert thought that he might work to help organize a Cub Scout pack of boys the age of his son. For several years there had not been one in his immediate community, and although he felt reluctant to take on the entire responsibility he was ready to lend a hand.

For his arrow labeled "sense of humor," he decided upon three promising possibilities. First was to use humor in public speaking, such as he might do if the motivational business training seminars worked out. Second was to use humor in his volunteer efforts as a counselor. He realized that this talent was a natural balance to the motivating, persuasive, organizing side of himself. Without the proper use of this important skill, his efforts might come out looking rather overbearing and pushy, which would not be fulfilling to himself or those he was trying to help. The third hypothesis was to get more involved in playful, fun-oriented activities with his family. He had an innate feeling for what would be fun and humorous. This expression would not only be a loving service to his wife and children but would also be a "Self"-nurturing thing to help keep him in touch with this individuality center.

As you consider the example of Robert's Step #3 and of

Amanda's which follows, notice one feature of how these hypothetical possibilities are written. A practical expression written in one rectangle may be an amended version of something you have written in another rectangle. In other words, some strengths, skills and aptitudes do not suggest expressions or manifestations of their own, so much as they qualify or give a special flavor to activities suggested by other talents of the soul. You can see this, for example, in the first two possibilities Robert recorded for his talent of humor.

Like Robert, Amanda—our other example—had four labeled arrows, and for each one she imagined new ways in which a particular talent of her soul might manifest as it expressed her individuality center.

For her arrow labeled "good with plants," she decided upon three promising possibilities. All three involved activities that would draw upon that strength, not so much in a direct service fashion, but in ways that were "Self"-nurturing. She wrote: "(1) expand my own garden; (2) take horticulture courses to learn more about plants; (3) spend more time out in nature."

For the arrow labeled "teaching," Amanda again had three hypotheses. First was to take a course or class to upgrade her public speaking abilities. Second was to offer classes herself on the topic of herbs. It was something she had specialized in for many years, but she had not attempted to share this knowledge with others. Finally, for this aptitude for teaching, she recorded the possibility of serving at the church by teaching some kind of class. She wasn't sure what topic would be appropriate, but she still felt that there were possibilities in this area of her life.

For her talent to be "innovative," she wrote two hypotheses for testing. Both of them were amended versions of possibilities she had already recorded. Her skill at being innovative offered her the chance to do these two things with a special "flavor" to them. First, she wrote that as she expanded the size of her own garden, she would try to find ways of growing herbs that don't easily grow in her locality. Second, as she offered classes on herbs, she would design new ways of presenting lecture and workshop material on this topic. Her feeling was that her soul talent for teaching would bring real fulfillment only if it were coupled with this other strength of being innovative.

For her fourth arrow, labeled "playful nature," she wrote two promising possibilities with which to experiment. The first was to get more involved with children. She thought this might include teaching children about nature and how to grow things, but she didn't want to limit it to just that. Her feeling was that she could serve children in ways other than she had been doing. This very talent of hers—to be playful—was one that allowed rapport to be quickly established. Amanda's second possibility for this talent was another one designed primarily to be nourishing of her individuality center. It was to get involved in a clowning group. She knew that in her community there were occasional workshops offered in clowning and that an informal group of workshop graduates met periodically to keep up this activity. Amanda's feeling was that such an expression of her aptitude for a playful nature would be very helpful in keeping her less identified with her personality wheel.

With these examples in mind, it is time now for you to work on your answers to Step #3. For each of the arrows you have labeled on your soul's purpose diagram, write between two and four possibilities in the appropriate rectangle. Keep in mind the suggestion that most of the hypotheses you record will fit into one of two categories: (1) new ways of serving others (or perhaps new versions of ways you have already been trying), and (2) activities that help you to stay in touch with a sense of personal identity which comes from your individuality center.

On a separate piece of paper, you may want to brainstorm a list of possibilities for each rectangle which is far longer than just four entries. You might want to engage one or more friends in this kind of creative imagining. From the longer lists, you can then pick the ones that feel most promising to you. Keep in mind that at Step #3 anything you record is still just an hypothesis. None has been tested yet, and you won't yet know if specific possibilities are really part of your soul's mission for this stage of your life. The testing and the deciding will come in the next step.

Step #4: Test the hypotheses through application. In Step #3 you will have created a list of many possibilities, many activities which may be a part of your soul's mission. However, simply through logic you cannot determine which of these possibilities are in fact part of what your soul intends for you at this point in your life.

The key to a research-oriented approach to self-discovery is *application.* Only through testing do you discover what is and what is not appropriate. This fourth step is based on the following assumption: Life itself will give you feedback on the appropriateness of an activity if only you will set in motion the first few stages of that hypothesis. In other words, if you will "get the ball rolling" and then watch for signs, you will quickly see which possibilities are part of your mission for this time in your life.

Seen from a logical perspective, one particular possibility may seem to be a definite part of your soul's purpose at this time. However, sometimes your personality will be surprised at the results of this fourth step of the process. As soon as you set that activity in motion, you may find that there are clear signs to discourage you from pursuing it further. Life itself is showing you that at this point in your life the hypothetical activity is not really in keeping with the way in which your soul's purpose wants you to invest time and energy.

What you are likely to find is that for some of your possibilities, there is a natural flow to how they unfold. As you set in motion the first stages of their application, there is a rhythm and synchronous pattern of progression to these activities. You find yourself in the right spot at the right time. A needed resource appears just at the proper moment. There are coincidences or synchronistic events to reinforce your interest in this hypothesis. Life is encouraging you to proceed.

All of this is not to say that the living of your soul's mission will be without obstacles. Even those activities which you are meant to be doing at this point in your life will have resistances which challenge you. However, the hypotheses which have a "rightness" to them will also provide signs of support and encouragement in spite of whatever problems or difficulties are also there.

To complete Step #4, proceed in this way. Work on applying your hypotheses from Step #3 one at a time. If you were to try to apply them all at once, it would be difficult to sort out the many signs that might occur in your life. For each hypothesis, set in motion the first two or three steps that are required of you to get things going. Make inquiry calls, look for the resources that would be required, search out the information you will need, talk to contact people who might help you be successful with this possibility. As you are doing this initial work of application, keep very alert for indicators. *The surest sign that an hypothesis isn't right for your soul's mission is not so much the presence of obstacles as it is the lack of any positive reinforcement signs.* Look for these signs in your dreams and intuitive feelings; look for them in unexpected things that people say or the way that events unfold; even look for them in the feelings or health of your body.

By way of example let's consider some of the aspects of how this step proceeded for Robert and Amanda. When Robert tried to set in motion the hypothesis regarding helping teenage boys, there were immediate signs of reinforcement. A local boys' club responded with enthusiasm to his inquiry. Although Robert had expected them to be receptive to a call from anyone offering help, they seemed to be genuinely excited about how his background fit their needs especially well. There was also a positive indicator in the timing of his inquiry. It coincided with the beginning of a new project they had planned. There were some obstacles, however. Robert had to rearrange parts of his regular schedule in order to be available when they needed him; but the positive signs certainly seemed to be stronger than the impact of these difficulties.

However, for another hypothesis related to his "motivator" talent, the course went quite differently. At every turn things seemed to go wrong when Robert tried to arrange business training seminars to motivate people. Sponsoring organizations either ignored his overtures; or, in the case of one that was interested, there was a series of misunderstandings and missed phone messages which kept the initial seminar from getting scheduled. There seemed to be clear signs about this possibility. Even though it logically appeared to be an activity which would be fulfilling to Robert and allow him to serve others, it wasn't really part of what his individuality intended for this time in his life.

One hypothesis for his "harmonizer" talent went very well when he applied the possibility. He tried some small scale ways of getting involved in personnel type work at his company. He had immediate success with helping several employees to better harmonize their abilities with the work they were asked to do. Even with these successes there were problems: His personnel manager felt threatened and insecure by what he saw as an infringement by his boss. But with some focused efforts at better communications between the two, even this was able to be resolved in a way that made the manager feel good about his job.

However, for his other hypothesis for the "harmonizer" talent, there were no encouraging signs. Robert made many inquiries offering to serve as a communications consultant to neighborhood businesses. But in every case his overture was rejected.

Only one possibility related to his talent of organization had positive reinforcement: helping to start a Cub Scout pack for boys his son's age. Despite some early problems in getting enough adults to help, too, plans for getting this activity started proceeded with a natural flow. A meeting place was found at no expense and the recruitment of boys exceeded expectations. However, none of the other hypotheses related to this talent had positive results when tested. Robert made some initial attempts at organizing his thoughts about business and management principles into a book or article format, but he wasn't satisfied with the product. As he made these preliminary efforts over a period of two or three weeks, he was never able to get a sense of rightness about this activity.

In a similar way, the other possibilities for this talent did not have a natural flow nor did they stimulate reinforcing signs. For example, his overture to the church leadership to serve as the treasurer was misinterpreted. The woman holding the position of treasurer at the time thought that this was Robert's way of saying that he had no confidence in her abilities. In the midst of this controversy, he felt obliged to withdraw his offer and look elsewhere for a way to serve with this particular talent.

However, two of his hypotheses related to "sense of humor" were immediately productive. In his volunteer work of counseling teenage boys, he found that a playful sense of humor was a major asset in his ability to relate to them. In this case, the talent was being used to augment a way of service that had been more directly suggested by one of his other talents. There were many, immediate confirming signs as he applied the hypothesis related to his family. It quickly changed the tone of his relations with family members, and life with them took on a new feeling of fulfillment.

In our other example, Amanda, there was an even greater frequency of successful applications of possibilities. In fact, from among the hypotheses she wrote, only one did not produce reinforcing signs. Her efforts to use teaching abilities at her church were, at least for the time being, rebuffed. There was apparently no need for new teachers at the time she made inquiries, although Amanda's intention remained to look into this possibility again at a later time.

At first, she had difficulties finding a group of children with which to work, even to which she might give classes about nature and plants. Yet despite these outwardly discouraging signs, she kept getting inward reinforcement. She had several dreams in which she experienced being with children in a positive interaction. In her own meditation life she continued to get a strong sense that this was something she was supposed to be doing. Finally, her persistence paid off and opportunities to be with and to teach children opened up for her.

The testing of her other hypotheses each brought confirming indicators. Both the works of service and the Self-nurturing activities she had chosen had a natural flow and unfoldment to them. Like Robert, she watched for certain feeling qualities to life which might be associated with these activities. These qualities were the universal characteristics described in the Cayce readings—inward signs we might all expect to notice as indicators that our actions are in keeping with our soul's ideal:

1. a sense of expanding awareness that brings with it the feeling of wonder and awe about life;

2. a feeling of closeness to others which comes from having given to them without expecting something in return;

3. a sense of greater wholeness, of being more complete, of being closer to God;

4. a deeper insight into how all of life is purposeful; and

5. a feeling of great joy.

Before moving on to the fifth and final step in this procedure, we might well address what you should do if most of your efforts at Step #4 do not result in confirming signs. As a sincere researcher, you must be open to this possible outcome. In such a case, the appropriate recourse is to go back to Step #3 and consider alternative possibilities. To do this, you might enlist the brainstorming help of other people, especially if you feel that you have already exhausted your own best ideas. The other alternative is to gó back to Step #2 and consider a different array of your talents and strengths. When such a block occurs at Step #4, it is often because the most significant talents, abilities and strengths for the soul's mission were not selected at the second step. With new talents chosen for Step #2, you would then proceed with new hypotheses for Step #3 and new efforts in application for Step #4.

Step #5: From among the successful tests, identify a theme that links them. Here is the step at which you try to formulate a succinct statement of your mission. Usually it will not be a direct statement about vocation, but instead a quality of consciousness or a certain way of going about life that you are here to manifest. Your talents and strengths make you especially well qualified to bring this into expression in the earth. The thematic statement of your mission may strongly suggest a particular vocational or avocational form. Or it may summarize a clear and specific mission, and yet be something which is also broad enough that it could be lived in a wide variety of vocational or avocational ways.

Take time to arrive at a unifying theme. Allow the wording to emerge as you progress with living some of your talents, strengths, and abilities in a new way. For some people, it takes considerable time to come up with one sentence which ties together what they are trying to do. You may be successfully living several aspects of your mission before seeing a thematic way they are linked.

Robert arrived at this statement for himself in Step #5: "To help and motivate the undeveloped to mature." He had found ways to live this purpose as a volunteer with teenage boys and Cub Scouts, with some of his employees at work, and in the way he began to treat certain parts of himself and members of his family. He realized that in the coming years this thematic mission might begin to express as new activities, things that were not yet appropriate for him while in his early 40s. He had found his mission, and yet there would continue to be an ongoing discovery process about how that mission would best be lived.

Amanda arrived at these words for her soul's purpose: "To celebrate the workings of God through nature." This is a very specific theme, and yet it is also broad enough that many activities fit its scope. Amanda found a deep sense of fulfillment in nurturing the "earthy" side of herself and in serving others through helping them be in closer contact with the Divine manifesting in the earth. She expected that in years to come this thematic statement of her mission would still be applicable, but with new challenges and opportunities.

Here are examples of other thematic statements of the soul's mission made by seekers using this five-step procedure:
- the appreciation of beauty
- to synthesize and blend
- the innovator: getting new things started
- to purify or to keep pure all I come in contact with
- sensitivity to the have-nots of life
- to be a builder, a finisher, to see things through to completion
- to be a spiritual inspirer through the arts
- to bring hope to others

The approach used in the preceding five-step process is largely a logical, rational one. It calls upon you to analyze yourself and to conduct personal experiments to arrive at conclusions. There are points at which intuition and feeling are helpful, such as in the selection of your spiritual ideal or the four key talents for your soul's purpose diagram. However, for the most part, a logical, analytical point of view is what is required.

Many who seek to know and live their mission in life find that such an approach needs to be balanced with ones which speak more directly from the soul. These supplemental approaches involve a more immediate contact with the unconscious psyche—with the soul itself. These are techniques which we might call the language of the soul. These approaches are called "supplementary" not because they are secondary in significance, but merely because the tone of this book has so largely been upon a logical, rational method of coming to understand your mission in life.

In many ways the language of the soul does not lend itself as easily to the printed word in book form as does the approach that is analytical. The language of the soul is fundamentally experiential, and you are invited to try one or many of its forms in your own life. As you experience these approaches, they are likely to stimulate new insights for you about key talents or even new ways of expressing talents which could be part of your mission. There are at least four broad areas of the language of the soul with which people have worked successfully to gain insights about their talents and their purpose.

In many ways *music* is the most readily available language of the soul. The Cayce readings speak of "music as the bridge," the bridge between the conscious life and the unconscious. Of course, much depends on the type of music chosen. But if you select music which has vibrations of harmony and higher attunement, then it may effectively stimulate in your mind creative insights related to your soul's purpose. You are invited to experiment with this: to try music reveries of 10 to 30 minutes in which you allow your imagination to respond creatively to the feelings generated by the music you have chosen.

What might you expect to receive from the music reverie? First of all, you should not expect that everything which comes into your imagination will be a profound insight into your soul's purpose. However, if you have selected uplifting music and if you enter into the experience prayerfully and with sincerity, then many of the images and impressions you receive can be very helpful. Some of them may relate to patterns of your personality wheel which are especially potent blocks or obstacles to your mission. Other images and impressions may reveal to you a talent or possible activity related to your soul's purpose.

The music will create for you a variety of ways to feel about yourself. In other words, it will allow you to experience different senses of identity. It will also stimulate memories, which occasionally may be painful and may still be controlling you though they are unconscious. Other memories may be very positive ones which you need to remember in order to understand your mission. Some people report memories which they feel may have a past-life quality to them.

The music may stimulate certain symbols that come to your mind. It is also very likely that a dream-like story will emerge which follows the impressions of the music. With the symbols and the story you can work with interpretive methods much as you would with a nocturnal dream.

Another aspect of the language of the soul is *sacred movement*. The body itself is an expression of the soul, and through certain activities—such as sacred dance—profound inner experiences can be awakened. For example, in the Sufi tradition the dervishes have elaborate dance movements which can result in altered states of consciousness and insights from the soul. Gurdjieff developed a complex set of exercises called Movements, and Rudolf Steiner created a form of symbolic, sacred dance called Eurythmy. As a seeker, you may wish to explore one or more of these avenues. As with music, it can provide a nonintellectual approach for gaining insight about yourself and your destiny.

A third version of the language of the soul is through *visual art*. Although this can take many forms, one which is especially noteworthy is the mandala. Here we may speak of either creating one's own mandala or imaginatively and creatively meditating upon one which has been created by someone else. A mandala is a visual representation of inner wholeness. It is generally a colorful, symmetrical diagram which depicts in symbolic or abstract form one's inner state of consciousness. A mandala is to creative imagination what a mantra is to attuned thinking in meditation.

Carl Jung made an in-depth study of mandalas and often had his clients draw mandalas at various stages of the individuation process. An excellent example of this work is provided in Jung's article, "A Study in the Process of Individuation," found in Volume 9 of his *Collected Works*. Simply, the experience of drawing a mandala can give you an encounter with deeper processes of your soul. There is not a prerequisite of great artistic skill in order to attempt the creation of a mandala. A number of books have been published that have detailed information about mandalas and how you can work with them. One classic in this field is *Mandala* by José and Miriam Arguelles (published by Shambala in Berkeley, California, 1972).

Finally, the language of the soul may take the form of words, but not discursive, logical arguments. Instead, when the soul expresses through words, it is more likely in the form of *myth* or *parable*. It is a sad fact that the word "myth" has lost its true meaning in our culture and has come to be a synonym for "fallacy." However, nothing could be further from the truth—myth does not mean "error" but rather "profound truth which is universal." The ancient myths have stood the test of time and still fascinate something deep within us. They speak to archetypal patterns within our souls.

In a similar fashion, Jesus and other great spiritual teachers chose to relate their messages largely in the form of story and parable. Was this because the people around them were simple-minded and needed the message delivered in such a nonintellectual way? More likely it was because of the very nature of mythic stories and parables. They operate at a level of feeling and knowing in which it is difficult for the rational mind to intrude and dismiss their impact. Often the intellect does not know what to do with a myth or parable. It can refute the happenings of the story as scientifically impossible and yet that does not dispel the deeper, intuitive impressions left.

You are invited to explore one or perhaps all four of these methods. Certain approaches may be better suited to certain kinds of people, but probably at least one aspect of the language of the soul can have an important role to play for you. It can give you an additional way of coming to know your own individuality center. It may provide a way of stimulating further insight for you about a talent or about some element of your soul's purpose.

Chapter 5
THE MYSTERY AND POWER
OF YOUR WILL

There is no aspect of your soul that is more important to finding and living your soul's mission than your will. Through the awakening of the will, you may have a shift in identity from your personality wheel to your individuality center. Through the awakening of your will, you have the capacity to apply that mission. It does little good merely to know with the intellect what the mission is. That purpose in life must be put into expression, and that requires the frequent use of the will.

The notion of free will has fascinated philosophers and theologians for centuries. There has always been a sense that the will in some way has a key role to play in the fulfillment of humanity's purpose in the earth. However, the search to clarify that role has often become confused in a web of hair-splitting analysis, often amounting to attempts to explain away the will in terms of other categories, like the mind and energy. Historically, we have often missed the point of how essential and basic the will really is, how crucial its proper use may be to the living of one's purpose in life. Perhaps a constructive view of the will is best initiated not by further logical analyses but with a parable.

The Parable of the Hero's Journey

In a land far away in times long ago, there lived a certain young man named Aleron. He was a fine man of beautiful, strong physical features, with a kind yet firm manner. Aleron was a laborer in the fields. His parents had died some years ago and now he was alone in the world. However, he was not one to feel sorry for himself, but rather approached life with a sense of optimism and adventure. From deep within himself he knew that there was more to his destiny than merely working in the fields.

One day the call came. It was not the sort of call that others might have heard, but rather a call that at the same time came both from within himself and from without. From within it came as a beckoning to meet himself in a new way; from without it came as an invitation to a great test: a challenge in some distant place that felt both foreboding and inspiring.

And so he departed, leaving behind the few responsibilities and ties that he had in the town of his birth. He merely followed the road which his own inner compass selected.

After traveling for many uneventful days, Aleron came upon a great cave. The road which he been traveling led directly into the cave and he followed it in. Although he did not realize it, he had entered into a magical cave—the first great test along the pathway to which he had been called. He soon discovered that this cave had many inviting side roads, many tempting opportunities to divert his path and follow side tunnels, each of which offered some enticing promise. Each possible detour presented to Aleron an image from his past. Down one side tunnel he might have followed the image of his mother, appearing as she did when he was a small child. Down another tunnel there was the image of a great banquet table on which had been prepared all of his favorite foods. And so the images and temptations continued. But at each and every choice point, Aleron chose to stay on the main pathway and soon he emerged from the cave, having passed beneath and through a great mountain obstacle on his journey.

Traveling on for many more days, he then came to a second test. This time he confronted a great river. It was in the springtime and the river's current was deep and strong. No man had ever been able to swim the river at this time of year and many had died in the effort. But Aleron felt his calling even stronger than before, and he knew that he could not wait the many weeks it would take for the river to subside.

Knowing it was foolish to fight the mighty current of the stream, he built a kite of animal hide and sturdy tree branches. Waiting for a windy day, he then summoned all the strength of his legs into a swift run directly toward the river. Aided by the kite and the wind he leapt and soared, spanning the river below, and landed safely on the far side. The harmony of his ingenuity, his body's strength and the forces of nature had allowed him to pass the second test.

Others had watched his great accomplishment, and word quickly spread of this great man and his deed. Aleron journeyed on that day, not expecting that when he arrived at a nearby city all of its inhabitants would have heard of his feat. They greeted him as a hero. For many years they had awaited such a one to be their leader. Their king had died without an heir, and the people had waited patiently for a new king to reveal himself to them. Now they were sure it was Aleron.

For his part, Aleron was not sure. Was this the great calling to which he had been summoned? With reluctance he accepted their offer and became their ruler.

Everything within his sight was now at his command. Everyone was prepared to do his bidding joyfully. Any maiden of this city and its surrounding lands could be his for the asking. Any horse or home was gladly given by the people if only they knew of his desire. Yet Aleron came to realize that, in fact, this was not the goal of his long journey. At first, he found it hard to give up all that he had in this city and to move on. But when he began to grow ill, he realized that he could no longer stay. The power which he held in this city, even though it was used with great care, was keeping him from the real mission of his calling. The day he departed from the city and continued on was also the day on which his strength and health began to return.

The third test had been passed. But now there lay before him the final challenge—the one to which he had been truly called. As the road carried him farther and farther into lands where no man had gone for many years, he came upon the domain of a great dragon. The dragon had been expecting his approach. It had long anticipated the journey of Aleron because of the treasure upon which the dragon sat. Aleron did not know of the treasure, but had he known what it was the dragon guarded he would have understood why this mysterious inner and outer calling had come to him.

A fierce battle ensued. Aleron fought bravely to defend himself from the attacks of the dragon. His sword and shield deflected many thrusts of the dragon's claws and many blasts of the dragon's fiery breath. But soon Aleron discovered that he could little hope ever to win this battle. The dragon had a magic power. Each time Aleron would pierce its thick skin, the dragon would grow even stronger. Each time Aleron would slice with a sword a scale or a claw from the dragon, two more would grow back in its place.

There was no chance of escape. Though Aleron now realized that there was no hope of his slaying the dragon, that same inner knowing that had first called him along this journey now told him that the dragon must die. There was only one way for this to be done. Aleron knew that by surrendering himself and allowing himself to be eaten by the great dragon, it would be poisoned and would die. Without fear, he accepted this solution because something within him—that same something that had first called him to this quest—whispered that his surrender would be a mysterious birth.

Aleron ceased to fight. The dragon, at first startled, drew back expecting a trick. Then it cautiously approached Aleron, and once within range snatched him and devoured him in one quick movement. But no sooner had the dragon swallowed Aleron than it fell and died.

At the moment of the dragon's death, the treasure was set free. In the lair of the dragon there was a cage in which was entrapped a woman. She was a person every bit as beautiful of body and mind as had been Aleron. In fact, she was the twin sister of Aleron, who had been stolen by the dragon when she and Aleron were but infants. Their parents had held no hope for her safe return and, presuming her to be dead, had never burdened Aleron with the story of her short life with them. It was her soul that had beckoned to Aleron to this journey. Now with the death of the dragon, the door to her cage swung open and she was free.

Emerging from the lair of the dragon, Kendra (for that was the name her parents had given her) saw the dead dragon before her. Now it was Kendra who heard an inner calling, an inner voice giving her instruction. This inner knowing told her to take the sword which she saw beside the dragon, cut a piece of his flesh, then cook it and eat it. This she did.

As she ate the flesh of the dragon, she also ingested the essence of her now dead twin brother. Into her mind there came the memories of everything her brother had ever experienced. She knew of his journey and of his decision to surrender himself to the dragon. She knew of all his experiences and hopes and dreams throughout his life. It was as if her brother were now alive again in and through her. But Kendra was also still herself. It was as if the essence and hopes of both their souls now lived in the earth through her body.

Kendra now set off on her own journey. She returned to the great city where for a short time her brother had been king. When she told the people of all that had happened and when the people saw her beauty and her wisdom, they proclaimed her their queen. There she ruled for the rest of her life with a power always tempered by the humility and self-surrender shown by her brother.

Our Birthright of the Will

This parable tells of the journey that each of us as souls has undertaken. It is a story in mythic images of our quest to find our true identity. Although the main character of the story is initially a man, the themes and patterns depicted in the parable are relevant to men and women alike, for none of us as souls is really male or female alone, but instead we each have an androgenous quality which integrates these two poles.

In the minds of some, this version of the hero's journey myth is an inferior one because the hero succumbs. In fact, Jung goes to great lengths in his writings to point out that an early format for this myth involves the death and then miraculous reappearance of the hero. He felt that this version preceded the modern development of self-reflective consciousness and that this early version depicted a process that was tempting but should be avoided: to give up and to lose one's identity in the unconscious.

However, a case can be made that this argument is not the best one to follow in evaluating the mythic story just related. On the one hand, we should note that the life of the Christ as hero includes an element of surrender (e.g., "resist not evil," and His very crucifixion). Furthermore, it would seem that we must distinguish between types of surrender. There is one variety that has a quality of despair and even self-destructiveness to it. We are all familiar with a small taste of it on those certain nights when we are so exhausted and discouraged that all we want to do is fall asleep and "forget it all." But there is another kind of surrender that is coupled to a higher ideal. It is an effort to offer oneself up so that something bigger and *more* conscious can emerge. It is to this second type of surrender that this mythic account belongs.

In many ways this is also a story about the human will and the journey that each of us is on to progressively awaken and claim the birthright of the will. From our creation as souls we have had access to three great components or factors of our being: (1) the spirit or the life force, the pure energy that is a spark of God within us, (2) mind, and (3) will.

Much has been made of the importance of the mind, and rightly so. "Mind is the builder" is a helpful phrase to orient us to the creative capability of the mind. But mind is more than just the builder. The mind also has the tendency to be the repeater, storing and replaying thought and emotional patterns from the past. A tape recorder is a good analogy for the mind: its dual functions parallel the workings of the mind. On the one hand, it is possible to record new impressions on the recorder's tape—to build a new image on the tape. On the other hand, it is possible to play back again and again the familiar sounds which have been recorded in the past. Most of us are inclined to use the playback function of our tape recorders more often. In a similar fashion, we are more inclined to use the "repeater" function of our minds much more often than the "creative builder" option. Here the phrase "creative builder" is carefully chosen because, in a sense, the mind is always building—but only rebuilding and reinforcing the old patterns when the mind is playing back and repeating the past instead of being creative.

In recent years, especially in the last two decades, there have been many breakthroughs in our understanding of the mind, particularly in the field of mind research and in explorations of altered states of consciousness. To a large extent, the cutting edge of the so-called "consciousness movement" has been a deeper and deeper probing of the nature of mind. The frontiers of the way in which we "do spirituality" in our society have come from this arena. We have mapped the characteristics of the unconscious; we have discovered the amazing, hidden resources of the mind to obtain knowledge through extrasensory means and to be a catalyst for healing. No doubt there is much, much more yet to be discovered.

However, the mind is no longer the frontier. It is not for lack of uncharted regions to explore, but because of a need for balance. There are two great faculties with which we, as souls, have been endowed and which give us a way to work with the life force we call spirit. In addition to the mind, there is the will. The evolution of human consciousness can progress only so far in the development of one of these faculties, until the demands of equilibrium require that progress be made on the other front. In the next two decades, we must make as much headway in understanding the will and tapping its potential as we have done in the previous 20 years with the mind. This is not to say that mind research will suddenly stop. Undoubtedly in the coming years there will be many more remarkable discoveries about the mind. Instead, it is a matter of where the truly crucial developments are taking place, and this shall be in the realms of the will. For, in fact, without further development of the will we are incapable of making constructive use of the remarkable findings of mind exploration.

In many ways the current situation resembles a time in history when fantastic, revolutionary discoveries about the geography of our planet were being made. Pioneers were bringing back information about new places where citizens of Western Europe might live. But there came a point at which, even though there were still undiscovered lands and uncharted regions, the cutting edge of what was most significant shifted. Now what became important were the methods of getting large numbers of people to the new lands and the ways of helping them sustain life in those new homes. So, too, in our own 20th-century situation, in our concern not about geographic exploration but instead spiritual development, it is time for this shift in emphasis. The often-forgotten faculty of will can now be appreciated anew and recognized as being equally worthy of development.

The will is the mainspring of our existence. The divine gift of will is that which makes us unique souls. Without will, none of us could be aware of ourselves as being ourselves, for the will is that which individualizes us and allows us to take on a particular sense of identity.

However, the will has rarely been appreciated in this fashion. It has been ignored or misunderstood, most often equated with a Victorian notion of "willpower"—which, in fact, is only one expression of will and not a very powerful one at that. The will has been simplistically dismissed as merely that function or capability which allows us to choose. Admittedly, there is a selecting feature to the way the will works, but it is far more than just that. Those people who prefer to limit their consideration of will merely to the label of "choice maker" should at least be prepared to examine exactly what it is that the will makes choices about. Any careful study of human behavior will reveal that most of what may initially feel like free-will choices which we make in daily living are in fact highly conditioned actions—they are decisions and selections we make under the strong influence of subconscious mind patterns and are not from the will. Where, then, in our lives does this so-called "choice maker" really operate?

Furthermore, is there an androgenous quality to the will or is it merely masculine in nature? Is it essentially "willpower" and self-assertiveness? Or is there an archetypically feminine feature to the will? In other words, is the will receptive or intuitive at any level of its development? The "Parable of the Hero's Journey" suggests answers in symbolic forms to these and other questions about the development of the will and its role in the spiritual quest. In many ways, the images of the story are more eloquent than any rational, logical explanation of these matters. But perhaps a more analytical approach to the subject can be viewed as a complement to the parable's evocative power.

The Development of the Will

One of the most significant breakthroughs in understanding has been the discovery in recent times that the human mind can best be worked with in a multilevel system. Rather than treat the conscious mind as if it were the entirety, we know from findings in the past 100 years that the mind is best understood as layered or existing in distinct stages. We might well ask ourselves whether or not the same kind of perspective on the will would prove to be fruitful.

What can we learn from clinical and experimental research into levels of the mind and altered states of consciousness? If we think of these distinct stages of mind as being somewhat like developmental steps in our work toward spiritual enlightenment, are there analogous steps in the development of the will? Our search for meaningful parallels can begin with a look at the specific stages of the mind.

On the one hand, there is a oneness to mind. Any attempts to categorize it or compartmentalize it may tempt us to forget this underlying unity. This temptation is well illustrated in the way in which we think of ourselves overall: as body, mind, and spirit. As helpful as it may be to conceptualize the human being in such a triune way, it can become a stumbling block to greater understanding if we forget that body, mind, and spirit are inherently coordinated and intertwined. In a similar fashion, the classic distinction of three levels of mind—conscious, subconscious and superconscious—has proved to be very helpful but is potentially misleading. We are not dealing with three different minds, but instead with three ways in which mind is experienced. As we develop a model of the will which involves several stages in its development, we are speaking of several different wills as much as several different ways in which they can be experienced. Just as there is an order of approach in our exploration of the mind (i.e., beginning with the conscious mind, then moving into the subconscious layers, and finally to the superconscious mind), we may well expect that an orderly developmental approach to the will shall be evident.

But how many developmental stages are there for the will? Should we assume "three" merely because the model of the mind we have used in recent times has three stages? Instead, it may well be that in our times a four-part system more readily matches the needs for understanding. Carl Jung has proposed that the transition in which humanity now finds itself can, from one point of view, be seen as a movement from models of a trinity to models of a quaternary. For example, the Christian trinity of Father, Son, and Holy Spirit might well add the missing feminine component of divinity—in whatever form or label one wishes to employ. In the same way, certain research with altered states of consciousness can be interpreted to suggest that for our times a four-part rather than three-part model for the mind may be more helpful. In this instance, the subconscious mind could be viewed in a dual role. On the one hand, a subconscious is oriented toward physical, conscious life; and on the other hand, a subconscious is oriented toward the spirit. Anyone who has carefully studied his or her dreams has, no doubt, directly experienced this distinction.

The First Stage of Development

In a four-stage developmental sequence for the human will, the starting point should be seen as the lack of will. We might think of this as being stage zero. Technically, a person who is at this stage does not lack the will, since this is a birthright of every soul; but rather, he or she has not awakened the will to any significant degree. The tiny amounts of the will's potential which *have* been awakened shall all be required to get the person moving along a developmental pattern.

This stage zero point can be thought of as sleep—not merely literal sleep but the metaphorical sleep in which we live our lives most of the time. For most people, the great faculties of the soul slumber while they are in the physical dimension of life. Stage zero with its almost total lack of will can be characterized as a highly subjective state. When we are in a subjective state, we are "subject to" the forces and influences from our environment. It is that set of outside factors which controls our experience.

Consider two examples of subjectivity. Suppose that a woman is asked to be the judge at a high school art show. The evaluation of art is already something which is highly idiosyncratic and given to personal differences in taste, so the woman in our example already has a difficult task in being the kind of "objective" critic that we would hope for in the judgment of any contest. But suppose that our story is further complicated by the fact that her own son has entered a painting in the competition. Seeing the look of hopefulness in his eyes and feeling the influences of her own maternal emotions, it may be very hard for her to make a truly objective decision. She may well be accused of great subjectivity in her choice.

Another example is the normal kind of dream that we have at night. Unless one is lucid in the dream (i.e., knowing one is dreaming while the dream is still going on), we can think of the dream state as being one of great subjectivity. In a dream one tends to simply react to what is going on; one is subject to the influences which are portrayed in the dream events. We may occasionally make what seem to be choices but even these are largely just reactions which are conditioned by the events and forces of the dream environment.

In considering the example of a dream, we might ask ourselves whether or not the various symbols and situations of a dream are really the "environment." Aren't these images really internal? Since they come from oneself, is one really being controlled and influenced by outside forces? Is one really in a state of subjectivity? The answer is still *yes*; subjectivity can be produced by influences arising from one's own mind. This crucial point is best made by distinguishing among three terms: awareness, mind, and will.

Let us think of awareness as pure consciousness—that within us which makes us a unique soul and which knows "I am that I am." By the term "awareness" we do not mean "states of awareness" or "states of consciousness," but rather pure awareness itself.

Then let us think of mind as being an "active force" which presents to awareness the contents of experience: how I feel, what I think, what I see, etc. It is somewhat like a movie screen on which is presented thoughts, images, feelings, memories, etc. However, in using the analogy of a movie screen, we must remember that the contents of an actual experience presented by mind are far more than just visual.

To complete our distinctions, let us think of will as an "active principle," which gives awareness a particular sense of identity. To the extent that the will has been awakened, a certain amount of freedom is given one to choose a particular sense of "who am I." Also, to the extent that the will has been awakened, more and more possibilities for the character of that sense of identity become available. With little or no will awakened, one is rather stuck with the sense of identity which is being presented by the mind (in an external way by the sights and sounds and impressions of the outside world; in an internal way by the overwhelming memory patterns of mind which come as attitudes and emotions). This is what we mean in saying that with little or no will, one is in a subjective state— subject to what the mind presents.

How do these three fundamental factors interrelate? In the course of human experience, how do awareness, mind, and will interact? Most simply put, it is in this fashion: The contents of experiences are received by awareness from the mind, and then awareness measures the experience against its own sense of personal identity. Recall that will is an active principle which gives awareness a particular sense of identity. This process can be illustrated in the following hypothetical situation of life.

Imagine you are at a business meeting in which a difference of options is being expressed by the participants. The ideas which you have expressed, ideas which you feel are very good and quite insightful, have not been accepted by the group. In this case, your mind presents to your awareness the contents of an experience. Those contents are both external (i.e., the sights and sounds of people rejecting and ridiculing your ideas) and they are internal (i.e., the mental reactions of humiliation, irritation and anger which automatically arise from the subconscious mind because of events in your past).

What happens next? Your awareness measures all these external and internal impressions from the mind against your own sense of identity at that moment. If your sense of identity is "the one who always knows best," then you will measure and respond one way; if your sense of personal identity is "the newcomer who is just learning how the business works," then you will measure and respond in another way. There are obviously many other possible senses of identity, and each would lead to a distinct way of your awareness measuring this experience and responding to it. Some senses of identity would lead to loving and patient reactions; others would lead to fear-based responses.

How awakened is your will? If you are at stage zero of development, with little or no will awakened, then from this highly subjective state you have surrendered to your mind all control of your response. If the will is active, there may be some choice in that moment of your individual identity and hence your reaction.

This hypothetical situation leads us to the first stage of development: the initial awakenings of will. Here we find the beginnings of self-reflection. At stage one the person starts to feel that his personal identity is not necessarily equivalent to what the mind is presenting at the current moment. The person begins to distinguish self-identity (i.e., "Who am I?") from what is mentally experienced as specific emotions, attitudes or impressions from others and from the physical environment. As elementary as this may sound, most of us spend very little of the day with the will awakened to even this first stage. Instead, we tend to remain "asleep," allowing the mind's presentation of the events of daily life to wholly shape who we feel ourselves to be. If you doubt this, observe yourself carefully for a day, even for an hour. You will notice how often your sense of "I" changes.

This first degree of awakening is not easy. It is a tenuous hold that we first have upon this birthright called the will. Because the movement out of sleep, out of subjectivity, is so difficult, the early awakenings of will are rather crude and even negative in character. But isn't this true of most beginnings? Our early efforts to walk were awkward and poorly controlled; our initial attempts to feed ourselves were messy. In a similar way, the first stage of will development is a sort of negative will: the capacity to say "no." For this reason we might label this stage of will the "negating will."

Will at the first stage attempts to forge a new sense of personal identity by rejecting the impressions presented by the mind. It takes on a variety of appearances: rebellion, negation, even the Victorian "willpower" or the capacity to reject temptations presented by the mind. In the "Parable of the Hero's Journey," the trip through the cave was a test to make sure that this level of will had been awakened.

To put another label on this stage of development, we might call it "adolescent will"—not because it is uniquely characteristic of teenagers, but because the images of the young person trying to form his or her new sense of identity apart from parents and family illustrates well the process. Imagine a 15-year-old boy who is getting dressed up to go out on a date. He puts on his brown suit and grey tie, only to have his mother come in and suggest that his brown tie would look better. We all know what typically follows. Even if the boy inwardly recognizes that his mother is "right," it is more important to him that the newly emerging integrity of his own personhood be respected. Using will at the first stage he rebels, he says "no" to her suggestions. Here the will has been used to distinguish between his own needs and identity versus what his mind presents to him: the sights and sounds of his mother, and the memories of his childhood past where she was the authority.

In the previous example of the business meeting, we can imagine how will at the first stage would manifest. What is it to which the will can say "no"? One possibility is to reject the perceptions made by the mind of what others in the meeting are saying. As your awareness receives from mind the sights and sounds of others rejecting and ridiculing your ideas, your will at the first stage of development could become an active principle, saying "No, I will not adopt the self-image to which these impressions would lead me; I know my identity to be something else." Another possible way that your will might operate is to reject the automatic responses that your mind comes up with, perhaps the attitudes and emotions of humiliation, irritation and anger.

With stage-one will there is a quality of repression inherent in negating the influences from the mind. If stage one is followed by further will development, this sort of repression can be healthy because it allows the experience of a clear feeling of unique personhood. However, if you never go any further than "willpower," such repression is likely to be detrimental. Stage one is a positive step in the use of the will to the extent that it allows you to dis-identify from patterns of mind that have been controlling your sense of personal identity and your responses to life. This kind of negating allows you to stand apart from old patterns of mind and create a new sense of yourself.

We all have personally meaningful expressions of how first-stage will manifests in our lives. For one person it is that which says, "I am not going to eat another piece of that pie which my mind is telling me would taste very good." For another person it is that which says, "I am not going to give in to that old feeling of resentment which my mind is telling me is the appropriate way to react to this individual." An effective self-observation exercise for each of us is to watch for the ways in which these first-stage stirrings of will awaken and manifest in our lives.

In one of the few books written on the topic of the will, Dr. Roberto Assagioli discusses an expression of will that resembles what we have called "negating will" or "adolescent will." In *The Act of Will* he calls it "strong will," and it has the same characteristics just outlined: the capacity to assert in a generally negating way. But this ability to withstand outside pressures is not the whole picture of the will. Assagioli was the founder of Psychosynthesis, a system of spiritual techniques which emphasizes the importance of disidentification and a proper sense of personal identity. He understood that to equate will in its entirety with this first stage—strong will—was really just a caricature of real will. Further stages of development were required, steps that we can now pursue.

The Second Stage of Development

The will awakened to its second stage is more than just an intensification of qualities from the first stage. On the one hand, the second stage is characterized by a greater degree of self-reflection; but added to this are distinct new ways in which the individual feels his or her own identity and reacts to life.

What is meant by self-reflection? It is not merely preoccupation with oneself. Instead, it is self-criticism—not the guilt-producing kind of accusations we might think of, but more like the objective view of a drama or literary critic. Self-reflection is the capacity to achieve an inner split so that a part of oneself goes on with the familiar thoughts, feelings and actions, while another part observes. Stated poetically, it is a matter of "standing aside and watching self go by." At the second stage of will development, the capacity for such self-reflection is strengthened.

More important, the second stage is characterized by the ability to *blend and synthesize*. At stage one the integrity of one's individuality was maintained by rejecting and negating certain impressions received from the mind (whether the source of these impressions was internal or external). At stage two the sense of individuality has grown stronger, and it is possible to use will to reconnect with the inner and outer worlds presented by the mind.

In the "Parable of the Hero's Journey," the second test was a challenge to demonstrate mastery of this level of will development. A river which was impassable by means of willpower and personal strength confronts the hero. His response is to blend the forces of nature in the wind along with the strength and swiftness of his body. In this synthesis he was able to move on and continue his quest.

The second stage might be labeled "adult will," again not so much because all adults demonstrate this development, but because our idealized notion of what it means to be adult-like includes characteristics bestowed by this level of the will. The adult is expected to be able to create skillfully a blend of two factors. First, there is an inner knowledge of what one's own unique individuality wants and needs in the present moment. Second, there is the vast array of influences coming from others, the environment, and one's own attitudinal and emotional past. At stage one of the will, differences between these two factors were resolved by the second factor being rejected in favor of the first. But now a new means of resolution is possible.

"Adult will" skillfully blends the genuine needs coming from one's own individuality with the demands and expectations arising from what the mind perceives. The quality of skill is so fundamental here that Assagioli even uses the term "skillful will" as the label for this second stage of development. Will at the second stage incorporates the influences which arise from the outside or from one's own past while still moving toward the goal or aim. Skillful will has a strong enough connection with one's self-determined identity as an individual soul that it is not threatened or overwhelmed by contradicting influences.

What does the voice of stage-two will say within us—how does it feel? In the case of the tempting pie, it may express itself as, "I know that pie would taste good and I am going to have some—but not right now—at the appropriate time." Or, consider the case of the 15-year-old who is told by his mother to switch to the brown tie. We might expect that when a similar event occurs ten years after this first one, that the now 25-year-old adult would respond differently to his mother. Because his will is more awakened and he has a stronger, less vulnerable contact with his own unique personhood, he can skillfully blend the factors present. He might say, "Mother, you are right, that brown tie would look good with this suit. Next time I wear this suit, I think I will wear it. But tonight I am going to go ahead with what I think looks just as good."

In the instance of the business meeting, recall that you were hypothetically put in a situation where your ideas were being rejected. Skillful will might create this kind of response: "Perhaps there are some weaknesses in the plan I proposed. But I think there are some helpful aspects to it also. Help me amend it so that it will work."

Admittedly, each of these examples is a bit simplistic. Often life offers us challenges with much more complex issues in which pat answers don't work. But the principle remains the same in any situation we confront. There is a level of the will from which we can operate which does not require us to be stubborn or negative in affirming our sense of individuality. No doubt, there are times when stage-one will is the more appropriate stage from which to operate, but often the appropriateness is because of our own needs for development and growth—and not so much something inherent in the event. From time to time in our lives we need to cycle back to stage one. It is not a developmental step which is reserved for teenagers. In fact, if you carefully observe yourself, you shall likely see that in a typical day your will awakens and falls back to sleep many times. You will probably see that you spend most of the day at stage zero, some time at stage one and only brief peak moments at stage two.

Another label for stage-two will is the "redeeming, nurturant will." With your sense of unique personhood and individuality established by stage-one will, it is possible to go back and re-embrace those patterns of mind which you negated and repressed at stage one. In this fashion there is an archetypically feminine quality to stage-two will, in contrast to the active—even harsh—character of the more masculine stage-one will.

The "redeeming, nurturant will" is able to direct attention so as to find, within the patterns of mind previously rejected, *something* which is harmonious with the ideal. For example, the 25-year-old young man can now use stage-two will to embrace the mental patterns related to his mother's criticism. Stage-one will has made him strong in his sense of individuality and now he need not fear being overwhelmed by memories of his childhood and mother's authority. He is able to use stage-two will to find the essence of caring within his mother's behavior and respond to it rather than to the strident form her criticism takes.

124

Just as some people have assumed that stage-one will was the whole picture of this faculty, there are those who have a broader view (which includes the kindness, cooperativeness and sensitivity of stage two), but then assume that is the end of the matter. But perhaps there is more. If we broadened our scope still further, two additional stages yet remain.

The Third Stage of Development

A dramatic change takes place with the third level of development. Up until now, the relationship among awareness, mind, and will has had a consistent character. The mind has been the "senior partner" in the group. Now the will awakens sufficiently so that the balance begins to shift.

We can label this stage of development "empowering will"—something quite different from "willpower." With the will awakened to this third step, awareness recognizes that no influence of mind is stronger than the will. The feeling which is created says, "I am an identity—a being—that is quite independent of anything my mind may present to me for experiencing." With this recognition comes a tremendous sense of control and power over life.

This stage of development is demonstrated in a particularly effective manner by the experience of a lucid dream. This curious phenomenon consists of the awareness in a dream that one is, in fact, in the dream state. It is a fairly rare occurrence for most dreamers but one that is not easily forgotten because of its novelty and great impact. The term "lucid dream" has frequently been misunderstood to imply any dream that is especially clear; for example, one in which the symbols are straightforward and transparent, or a dream in which the interpretation is literally given while one is still in the dream. However significant those kinds of dream examples may be, they do not describe lucid dreams. Rather the term is used strictly for a special event that occasionally happens in our dreams: the recognition of dreaming while the dream is still going on.

What do such lucid dreams have to do with our study of the will? In a typical (i.e., non-lucid) dream, one is in a highly subjective state, with little or no will present. Even the dream experiences in which we seem to be making choices are probably more a matter of unconscious habit patterns, with mind doing the choosing. There is virtually no self-reflection or recognition of one's sense of individuality. But something very different takes place in a lucid dream: The will awakens.

With the introduction of lucidity, awareness recognizes that it has identity and individuality apart from the dream events. In saying, "This is merely a dream state," what is the dreamer actually asserting? He or she recognizes that this dream world is somehow or other distinct from at least one other world in which the dreamer has experiences, i.e., the normal world of physical life. For example, suppose that a person has this experience:

> I'm in a dark, poor section of a city. A young man starts chasing me down an alley. In the dream, I'm running for what seems to be a long time. Then I become aware that I am dreaming and that much of my dream life is spent running from male pursuers. I say to myself, "I'm tired of this never-ending chase." I stop running, turn around and walk up to the man. I touch him and say, "Is there anything I can do to help you?" He becomes very gentle and open to me and replies, "Yes. My friend and I need help." I go to the apartment they share and talk with them both about their problems, feeling compassionate love for them both.
> (From *Lucid Dreaming* by Scott Sparrow, A.R.E. Press)

In this dream, self-reflection awakens sufficiently so that the dreamer (a woman in this case) recognizes an identity apart from the images which her mind is presenting in the dream. In a typical dreaming state, she would have responded subjectively to the events of the dream, events which try to shape her identity as a pursued, fearful person. But with lucidity, the will acts potently to create a sense of individuality, which contrasts with the influences from the dream. From this new feeling of identity, she responds in a creative, loving fashion; and in return, the images of mind (i.e., the dream symbols of the men) alter their behavior and attitude.

This dream beautifully illustrates an effective use of will at the first and second stage, and then it concludes with will at the third stage: "empowering will." With the awareness and words, "I'm tired of this never-ending chase," the dreamer exhibits stage-one will by negating old mental patterns. With the decision to turn, confront and embrace that which was previously avoided and negated, the dreamer demonstrates the skillful, redeeming, nurturant will of stage two. Then, at the third level, mind becomes the servant of will, as demonstrated in the dream when the images and events change. Oftentimes, however, empowering will is not used in such a constructive manner. In fact, this third stage of development is a critical, even dangerous, point. The possibility and temptation arise to use the will to serve selfish or limited ends. In a lucid dream, the tendency is to use the new-found power of awakened will to manipulate the dream content. Such experiences are quite possible and available with this level of will. Most people who have had lucid dreams have discovered such remarkable capabilities. They find that they can escape from uncomfortable dream images by just flying away, or by wishing or willing the undesirable images of mind to change into something else.

In the example quoted above, the woman might have used her lucidity in a less constructive way. She could have turned to her pursuers and used her will to imagine them as friends or benevolent beings. No doubt, such dream manipulation would have taken place. But such a choice would have been to avoid something within her in need of healing—it would have been to disrespect the integrity of the dream. Admittedly, the dream images did change once her lucidity emerged. However, it was not because she tried to overwhelm the dream images of her mind with the power of her will. Instead, she used the power of her will to create a constructive, fear-free sense of her own identity, and then the dream began to change as a natural result.

What, we might ask, does all this have to do with daily living? The answer is that the process experienced in a lucid dream is very similar to what is possible in physical, conscious life. We can learn lucid living. It may not be experienced in daily life exactly in the way it is in the dream state. However, both involve the awakening of the will to this stage we call "empowering will."

When the empowering will emerges, a fundamental shift in perception takes place. In the dream state the perceptual shift creates the view that "this is only a dream" and, therefore, a feeling of invulnerability. In physical life the perceptual shift creates the view that the world presented by the physical, conscious mind is actually the past and not the present.

This recognition is a radical change in how we view life. At this third stage, not only has the balance of influence shifted from the mind to the will, but now the mind is experienced as the primary agent of the past. A careful analysis shows that this, in fact, makes sense, even though it is contrary to the way in which we are accustomed to seeing things. Our attitudes and emotions are patterns of mind which merely reflect our past experiences. When one feels angry or jealous, the emotional experience presented to awareness by the mind is largely determined by past events. The anger I may feel today is real; but its energy has been created and formed by circumstances in my past.

But not only are the internal attitudes and emotions recognized as being of the past, we also recognize that the external, physical world is the past also. On the one hand, this notion sounds nonsensical to our minds, but consider the implications of the universal law, "The spirit is the life, mind is the builder, and the physical is the result." That law simply states that everything which we experience as physical reality (e.g., our bodies, material objects, etc.) has been created first at the dimension where mind is the builder. Initially mind creates, and then later (perhaps seconds later or perhaps years later) the pattern of energy manifests in physical form. The findings of psychosomatic medicine illustrate this law very well as it relates to our physical bodies. Through our state of mind we build the relative health or dis-ease of our bodies. Our bodies are concrete, material expressions of our past. The law works in a similar fashion for other things we experience as physical reality.

The awakening of will at the third stage—empowering will—brings this recognition. Mind no longer has such a hold on us because we realize that the impressions brought to us by mind are images and influences of the past. They are real, but our tendency up until now has been to misinterpret them and to give them an unwarranted control in shaping our own sense of identity. Even with this level of awakening, the mind still functions as the builder, but it is as the servant-builder under the direction of the will. At this third stage will is an initiator, directing the building of new patterns of mind.

If mind is that which gives us impressions of the past, then what is the present? It is the sense of who we are which is selected by the will. For example, suppose you are at a dinner party and someone makes an insulting remark to you across the table. If you are metaphorically asleep, at stage zero of will, then you will react in a subjective way. Your inner sense of identity will be subject to whatever emotional pattern arises from your subconscious mind in response to what you have just heard. You may toss a similar insult back.

But if you have awakened your will to stage one, you may resist the inner emotional pattern and have the "willpower" to keep silent. At stage two you might find something to say or do which skillfully blends an appreciation for the other person's dislike for you along with the clear awareness that your real identity is not what the insulting remark implied. Perhaps this would be a good-humored comment which takes note of the feeling behind the other person's attack but at the same time proposes a different picture of who you are than the view he has been seeing.

However, at the third stage of will development another perspective is introduced. With empowering will you recognize that the feelings and comments of the other person are actually images of his past. What you are seeing and hearing is not really the present of that soul but rather a physical expression of experiences from his past. You also recognize that your own emotional reactions of outrage and resentment are patterns of energy arising from your own past. All of this is quite real, and yet the will allows your awareness to be in the actual present moment. The will allows you to select an identity for your individuality. Then, whatever response you do make will flow from the identity you have chosen and not from the one determined by your past.

To depict this in a model or diagram you can see that the mind is that which tends to draw you back to the past. Even its building and creating function has the *tendency* to recreate and reinforce patterns from the past. When the will is awakened, it draws you into the future. *When it is in charge and creatively directing the mind, movement toward your destiny and soul purpose is possible.*

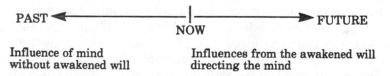

PAST ◄————————————|————————————► FUTURE
                            NOW

Influence of mind   Influences from the awakened will
without awakened will   directing the mind

The third stage of will development is a potentially dangerous one. It is particularly at this level that the will can be used to fulfill selfish aims rather than altruistic ones. With the sense of personal power it provides, the seeker can literally lead himself astray. Without a high ideal to keep himself directed, the influence of the will over the mind can get him even more deeply entrapped in a mistaken identity for himself.

For example, consider again the moment in which one becomes lucid in a dream. How is the will used in this opportune situation? Some people have suggested that dreamers should practice a form of dream manipulation in which the will is used to wish mentally things which have been desired but unfulfilled in daily life (e.g., to have a dream imagery affair with a sexually desirable person who is unobtainable in waking life). However, there is probably a great deal of wisdom lacking in such counsel. Such dream manipulation using empowering will creates patterns of mind which do not merely dissolve upon awakening from the dream. Such inner behavior is as unsound for personal ecology as is tossing trash from one's car window, thinking to be rid of it.

Stage three is the danger zone of will development because one can misunderstand this level, believing it to be the final step, the goal. If the seeker lacks the perspective of something still ahead—the transcendent—there is the temptation to use the power of this level to strengthen the desire patterns of the personality. Furthermore, a person who has awakened will to this level can have a remarkable influence over those other people who have not yet awakened the will, especially those who spend most of their time at stage-zero sleep.

One of the best and most tragic examples of this process is the life of Adolph Hitler. By all accounts of him, it seems that this man profoundly developed his will and with it a very distinct sense of his own identity. That will was able to withstand many forms of resistance to his chosen identity in the early years of his rise to power. In this rise to power, he seemed to have an almost hypnotic effect on the minds of others. Not only was Hitler's own mind the servant of his will, but the minds of others became servants also.

Perhaps because of examples such as this one, Assagioli calls the third stage of will development "good will." In this fashion he defines what is required if this third stage is to be a stepping-stone to the next stage, for without an ideal of goodness coupled to empowering will, we cannot hope to experience transpersonal will. However, "good will" is not assured at this stage; there is always the chance that the empowering will will be employed to the detriment of self and others.

In the literature of myth and fantasy, J.R.R. Tolkien's *Lord of the Rings* trilogy includes a symbol which resembles in many ways the empowering will. The ring itself is an image of great power and influence as well as the potential to be caught up in the dark side of power. The ring even provides its wearer with a hypnotic or mind-altering effect on others, because the wearer of the ring becomes invisible to all around him.

In the "Parable of the Hero's Journey," the challenge of this third stage of development is depicted by the hero's ascent to the role of ruler of the land. At first, he assumed that this position had all along been the goal of his calling. It gave him the personal power to have anything his mind showed him. But soon that became dissatisfying. He realized that even with all this power the deeper calling of his soul could never be fulfilled in this way. So he had to move on in his quest, to a point where self-sacrifice would be required.

The Fourth Stage of Development

Stage four is the Real Will of the soul, what Assagioli calls the "transpersonal will." In traditional religion this has often been referred to as the will of God. The two points of view are not incompatible because at this level the individual's will has aligned itself with the will of God.

What is required in order to move from stage three to stage four is surrender. What must be given up is the extensive personal power created by empowering will. We must also surrender a certain sense of our own identity, which up until now has still maintained a high degree of separateness from the whole. It is not that stage four makes us return to the oceanic feeling of oneness which we had at creation, a loss of unique individuality. Instead, it is a surrender in which our old, mistaken notion of unique, personal identity dies and what is resurrected is individuality as we have not previously experienced it. That new individuality knows itself to be itself (i.e., full self-reflection) and simultaneously knows itself as one with the universe.

This situation constitutes a subtle distinction often misunderstood about surrender, death and rebirth. The personality self is relieved to hear that in moving from stage three to stage four, the sense of unique personhood is not destroyed. But the personality self assumes that the sense of individuality which a soul has with stage-four will is still the same personality self. To the contrary, the personality dissolves. What is awakened is something resembling the personality in that it senses its own distinct (even separate) nature. However, this something new—this individuality in its full flower—is a quite different way of the soul experiencing itself and the universe around it.

How, then, are we to understand the experience of will at the fourth level? One of the most insightful of teachers about the will, Ouspensky, describes it to be like suddenly seeing the solution to a mathematics problem. No doubt, we have all had the experience of working intently on some abstract issue which we knew had an answer but seemed to elude us. Then, there may have come that instant in which we suddenly recognized the solution. In Ouspensky's system, the feeling of Real Will is much like that feeling associated with finding answers which work.

This analogy is an especially effective one because it reminds us that the universe is orderly. The mathematician trusts that his array of scattered observations can be combined into some formula because he knows the universe is lawful. In the same way, we struggle with the scattered challenges and difficulties of our lives. The experience of Real Will in relationship to those problems is the recognition of creative possibilities of how to respond in life effectively.

The Real Will or transpersonal will is that which reveals solutions. It does so by uniting the influences of life in order to create something new. The content of revelation from transpersonal will is usually a surprise to us; its solution comes as something not considered by the personality self—often even rejected at first by the personality because of its unexpected or foreign quality. But it is the feature of "new possibilities" offered by Real Will which gives it a power to transform us far beyond the influences of stage-three will. The answers and solutions proposed by empowering will are usually an extension of the personality we already are; transpersonal will reveals to us the invitation to be something more.

The process of experiencing stage-four will—and, in fact, all the stages of will development—is depicted in meditation. This spiritual discipline can be seen as a specific training procedure for the will. Typically, we begin at stage zero, going about our daily activities in a relatively sleep-like state of automatic reactions to life. When the appointed time of day for meditation comes, we start by using stage one of the will: a negating will which tries to keep the mind one-pointed upon the mantra or affirmation by rejecting any distractions. This is effective, to a degree, in moving us to a deep level of concentration. But far more is required if we are to meditate effectively.

Awakening the second stage of the will, we can begin using any distractions which arise to take us actually deeper into the spirit of the affirmation. Employing skillful will, we can blend the content of the distraction with the motivation or ideal of the affirmation. For example, suppose that one's affirmation was, "Let me be a channel of blessings to others." When a distracting thought arises about one's mother-in-law, there is an option other than using the negating will to force the distraction aside. Instead, the meditator can use the thought of this person to be a reminder of a place in his or her life where the ideal of loving service could be applied. The meditator might even take a moment to feel the channeling of blessings to the mother-in-law. In so doing, the meditator may experience deeper attunement.

Continuing this process, one comes to a point in meditation where the mind begins to get still. Instead of the recurring parade of images and memories surfacing from the unconscious mind, there is stillness. The mind has become the servant of the will. Will at the third stage has emerged. In this personally empowering state, much is possible in meditation. One feels re-energized and at the same time profoundly relaxed and at peace. However, this is the danger zone of meditation. In her classic book on meditative and mystical states entitled *Mysticism,* Evelyn Underhill describes this state of meditation as "The Quiet." She says of it that "The Quiet" tempts the meditator to believe that he has now arrived. The sense of personal expansiveness and personal empowering is dangerous if the meditator forgets that there is yet a further step: one that requires a letting go.

The highest state of meditation is one in which the Real Will takes over. Here there can be a revelation of the purposes and insights of the soul. Ultimately meditation is surrender. In the end the meditator can do nothing to make something happen, even with the considerable powers of stage-three will. There must come the surrender and the trust which allows a rebirth of our sense of identity.

In the "Parable of the Hero's Journey," the development of stage-four will comes in the confrontation with the dragon. Only as the personality of the seeker is willing to dissolve can the individuality be freed. Only when the hero surrenders himself is his twin sister able to truly live.

But the story does not end with the immediate rebirth or freeing of the heroine. There is a reintegration. The heroine eats of the dragon's flesh and the hero "lives" again, but now in a subservient role. His memories, hopes, and even his consciousness are resurrected, but they have life through the body and the will of his twin: the individuality of the soul. The parable teaches us that the work of finding and living one's soul purpose is not a matter of permanently destroying our present personality selves; it is instead a matter of making the personality more passive so that the individuality can come alive. In a similar fashion, even after the most profound of meditation experiences, we "come back down" and find ourselves to be personality again. But a subtle change may have happened. The deep meditation experience may have been so transformative that now the personality traits have become obedient to a more enlightened sense of identity.

This parable is a variation of the more traditional Greek myth of the hero. No doubt, we have all heard the myth in which the dragon is slain by the sword of the hero. In some of these versions the heroine in her dependent, passive role is rescued by the hero. But that version is a pre-Christian one. The essence of the Christ's message is that we must be reborn. The earth (i.e., the dragon) is not overcome by fighting it at its own level, on its on terms. The will which "saves" us or allows us to know and live our soul's purpose is a more receptive, intuitive feminine will. The assertive, power-oriented masculine will (especially seen in stages one and three) is not enough. Just as Jung felt that the time was ripe in human history to add a fourth element to divinity—moving from a trinity to a quaternary—it is also time to recognize the significance of this fourth stage of the will. Our tendency has been to recognize culturally the three masculine components of God (Father, Son, and Holy Spirit) or the assertive side of will. This "Parable of the Hero's Journey" teaches us that something more is required.

Finally, we might well ask, "Why not go directly to stage-four will?" In other words, why don't we begin our efforts to awaken the will by merely inviting God's will to work through us. In fact, we can; but only because it is possible to work on developing slowly all four stages simultaneously. But this does not mean we can bypass the first three stages. Before we concern ourselves with ultimate surrender, let us be sure that we have something of substance that we are offering up. Jung worked with his patients to develop a strong sense of individual nature (ego) before moving in the individuation process to transpersonal development. Assagioli's system teaches personal psychosynthesis before spiritual psychosynthesis.

The development of the first three stages is crucial because those levels of will allow us to function in the physical plane. When we have moments in which transpersonal will awakens, the accompanying revelation will always require an application. The Real Will reveals solutions, but then the solutions must be lived in three-dimensional expression. If we have not worked to develop adolescent/strong/negating will and skillful/redeeming nurturant will as well as empowering will, then the insights, solutions, and possibilities uncovered by transpersonal will shall not truly benefit us. It is an irony of the spiritual path. We must work hard to achieve something and then be prepared to surrender it. Many times it will be given back to us, but always we must be ready to surrender it again.

Chapter Six
A MODEL FOR
UNDERSTANDING YOUR WILL

The purpose of a model is twofold. First, it helps us organize our ideas about a topic. By systematically arranging what we know into a cohesive picture, we can get a better hold on what might otherwise be merely scattered observations. Second, a model helps us to predict, to look ahead and see what our future experiences may be. In physics or chemistry, a model of matter and natural laws can not only help the scientist grasp the meaning of his observations, but can also assist him in making hypotheses for future experiments. The same process can work for us in regard to our study of the will and its relationship to the mind.

No model can explain everything. For example, in drawing a two-dimensional diagram to summarize relationships among third- or fourth-dimensional items, certain important features must be lost. The very thing that makes a model handy—its simplicity—is also its limitation. In other words, we should not expect too much from any model. It is only natural that we find exceptions that don't fit the model, particularly when the model is trying to represent in the limitations of two dimensions the nature of a reality of far greater complexity.

With these reservations stated in advance, we can move ahead and explore the value of a model to depict the relationship between mind and will. The diagram we shall develop is based on the principle that mind and will are in direct opposition to each other. On the one hand, this sounds like a discouraging notion. It suggests that these two great components given to the soul at creation are doomed always to compete and to be at war with each other. It seems to imply that each of us is stuck with a kind of internal conflict that cannot be remedied.

On the other hand, there is a more hopeful way of viewing this principle. The many examples already given suggest the truth of this inherent opposition. There is a recurrent tension between mind and will to shape one's sense of personal identity. The mind tends to build and reinforce an identity shaped by past experiences. The will is an active principle which can orient one's identity toward the future, one's destiny in spiritual evolution. When the will is awakened and active, the mind is operative and is subservient to the will. Yet even then it retains the tendency to revert to the old and familiar patterns. If the will momentarily falls asleep, the mind shall take the lead again.

This sort of tension is part of the way we are built, but the tension can be viewed in a positive way: It is a creative tension. Just as there would be no electricity to cook our food or heat our water with positive and negative electrical forces, there might not be spiritual evolution for human souls without a creative polarity that can potentially be used to propel us forward.

So we construct our model of the mind and will by starting with this basic principle of opposition. It can be represented as two axes.

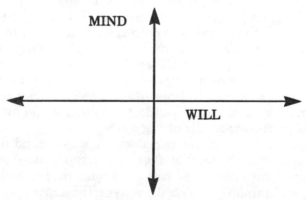

From high school mathematics you may remember drawing graphs of algebraic expressions which could be depicted on axes like these, although they were not labeled "mind" and "will." To illustrate how this two-dimensional skeleton of a model can be used to represent relationships and experiences, let us start with something far more mundane than the inherent tension of the human soul. Let us take the simple example of heat and humidity, something we become particularly aware of in the middle of the summer.

Suppose we label the horizontal axis "heat" and the vertical axis "humidity." Let us work with just the upper righthand quadrant of the skeletal model. In the summertime, we are not concerned with measurement of temperature less than zero; and values of humidity below 0% do not have a meaning.

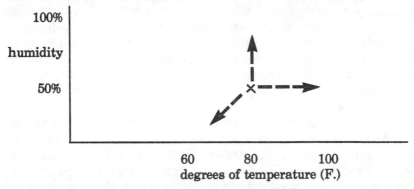

The "x" on the diagram represents the experience of being in a room with a temperature of 80°F. and a humidity of 50%. Each of the three dotted arrows depicts how our experience of heat and humidity could be altered. The horizontal arrow shows a movement on our model which is created by rising temperature with no change in humidity—which would happen in the room if we drew back the curtains to permit some solar heating. The vertical dotted arrow shows an increase in humidity with no change in temperature—which would happen if we sprayed a mist of 80°F. temperature water in the room. Finally, the diagonal dotted arrow represents decreasing temperature accompanied by decreasing humidity—which would happen if we turned on the air-conditioning system.

In a similar fashion, we can depict specific conditions of human experience. Instead of degrees of temperature, we shall be concerned with stages of will development. Instead of the percentage of humidity, we shall focus on the expansiveness of mind, ranging from unlimited, universal mind to the rather confined state of mind we call the three-dimensional, physical conscious mind.

In the diagram below, the axes are labeled and the points of measurement along each have been added. The indication of "∞." at the top of the mind scale means infinite or divine mind. The point labeled "3-D" means the three-dimensional, physical conscious mind. The unlabeled region in between represents various dimensions of mind which are not as limited as our typical conscious minds but which do not have the expansiveness of infinite mind.

138

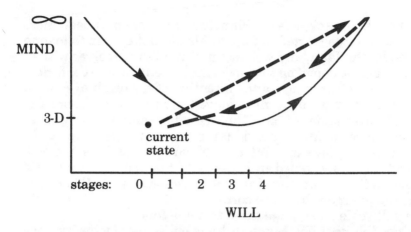

In this diagram two pathways are depicted. Each illustrates one of the interpretations of the story of our creation as souls and the journey of the soul's evolution. The dotted line shows the first, or more traditional, interpretation. It starts with a creation in which souls were given divine mind and a fully developed birthright of the will. Then, it shows that by a rebelliousness of will, souls entered more and more limited states of mind and ultimately began to lose access to the will as the limited dimensions of mind became more and more hypnotic.

The dotted line of this first interpretation shows that we arrived at a point of three-dimensional mind and relatively little will (on the border between stage-zero "sleep" and occasional awakenings of stage-one will). From here the dotted line shows a pathway back: the work of spiritual growth still ahead for us. It is a future of retracing our steps. From the perspective of this first interpretation of the creation story, the point of the journey we are on is to return to more or less the exact same state from which we began.

In contrast, the solid line expresses a second interpretation of the creation story. In this case, souls were created with infinite mind but the will was only an unawakened potential—like a present or gift that had been given but was yet unopened. Souls were one with God but they did not know it; it was unconscious oneness. The purpose of the soul's journey was to become something better. The soul had laid before it a plan whereby, through the awakening of the will, through the awakening of the sense of individual identity, it could become a co-creative companion with God.

The solid line depicts the Plan. It was a great purposefulness that each of us started out upon. We did not end up following carefully the Plan, and we must now realign ourselves with it. But before we depict on the model the current human condition, let us get a clear image of the intention of the original Plan. It shows that we were meant to move temporarily into more and more limited states of mind, but with an ever-increasing sense of our own unique, individual nature. A point would be reached—the lowest point of the parabola—where the will would be so awakened in a personal fashion that we might move yet another step into transpersonal will. (Note: the turning point on the curve corresponds to the transition along the will scale from stage three to stage four.)

Once the Real Will began to direct our sense of identity, then the higher states of mind would once more be attained. The goal of the journey would be a mind as unlimited and divine as that which we had in the beginning, but now with a fully developed sense of our individualities. Truly, we could then be co-creative companions with God.

It is this second interpretation of the story which we shall now pursue. Its basic assumptions and perspectives are those we have been using throughout our exploration of finding one's soul purpose. In the diagram below, the model has been altered somewhat to illustrate the error that souls made along the way. Like the first interpretation, this story claims that a mistake was made. However, the two interpretative stories differ in their theory of where the error or the "Fall" took place. In this first story, it was at the beginning, when the soul first made a movement toward a more limited state of mind. In the second story, it was intended that we experience limited states of mind, but an error took place when we continued to move toward ever more limited states of mind while starting to surrender rather than develop the will. Notice how the curved arrow shows this kind of movement: deeper into mental limitation but regressing in terms of a development toward the awakening of individuality.

We might consider what occurred in the following manner: Souls moved into limited states of mind in which they could more readily feel their individual natures. But in so doing, they found themselves in a place where they could use their newly awakening will to create mental images to satisfy selfish ends (i.e., just as a lucid dreamer today can choose to manipulate the dream images and create whatever patterns of mind seem

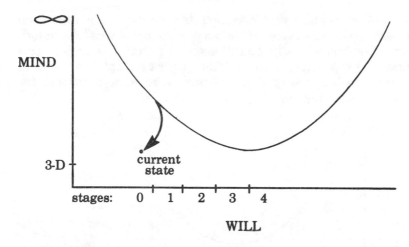

pleasing). But in so doing, they created images which began to have an hypnotic effect. The souls fell subject to what they had created, forgetting their individualities as souls and believing their identities to be something far less.

So we, as souls, find ourselves today in a peculiar state. We have descended into three-dimensional conscious minds and bodies. In a sense, we were meant to do so. There was a work for us to do here: to bring the qualities of spirit into matter, to make the infinite finite. However, when we reached this state of mind we were meant to have quite a different state of will. Our experience in matter has not turned out the way it was intended, largely because we now live in a sleep-like state (the great faculties of the soul, such as the will, are slumbering) and because we have a mistaken notion of who we are.

So we are left with the question of how to get back on the Path. Psychologically speaking, the Path is like a great stream of archetypal images and universal patterns of consciousness. The myths and parables which have a spiritually quickening impact on us are the ones which are attuned to this great psychic roadway. With the creation of a Divine Plan for the evolution of souls toward co-creativity, that Plan took the form of universal images within the unconscious of every soul. In a sense, they are like road markers to confirm for us that we are on the right track. Furthermore, their symbolic quality goes beyond just being confirmatory signs; they also contain a mystery or a tension which provides the energy to move on and evolve further.

What can we do to put ourselves back in the flow of that Path,

141

so that we actually experience the energy, the universal patterns, and the sense of its deep purposefulness? Although there are undoubtedly countless ways that the seeker can pursue the spiritual quest, four primary options present themselves from the model. They are depicted below in a series of versions of our model.

MIND

WILL

The dotted line represents a movement back onto the Path, which involves a lessening of will simultaneous with a heightened state of mind. What comes into awareness is an aspect of mind far less limited than the typical, three-dimensional conscious mind. But this is done at an expense. Awareness finds itself in a much more subjective state, in which the sense of identity one feels is determined by the content of these altered states of mind. Examples of such movements include psychotic experiences as well as the induced psychosis produced by hallucinogenic drugs.

The person having a psychotic episode is probably having genuine encounters with higher states of consciousness, perhaps in some instances encounters with the Divine. But the experience is of a highly subjective nature: the will is paralyzed. The content of the experiences may often have archetypal, mythic characteristics, but the psychotic finds himself stuck at this point and unable to integrate his experiences with three-dimensional life.

A similar thing can happen with LSD or other hallucinogens. A mental experience of greater dimensionality emerges, but it is at the expense of the will. While in the experience, the person can only sit back subjectively and react to what is happening.

Little or no control is possible. In a fashion, it is like playing roulette with one's sense of identity: one can be sure that he shall have thrust upon him a much more complex, intricate experience of who he might be, but one can never be sure of a "good trip" or a "bad trip."

This first option might be viewed as de-evolutionary. Admittedly, it *may* get the seeker back in the flow of the Path, but it moves him to a point far in the past. Hundreds of thousands of years ago, the human psyche may have been at a place very much like this. There are instances of people who are inspired by such experiences, who have such profound encounters with a higher state of mind that they are motivated to become seekers in a different and more effective manner. But there are also many instances of people who become psychologically addicted to the hallucinogenic experience. Unfortunately, the drug always wears off and one comes back down. With continual use, one is likely to find that the weakened, paralyzed will becomes a continual state of affairs. Even back in a three-dimensional conscious mind, the will becomes no more present than it was during the drug trip.

The second option for the seeker is depicted by a vertical dotted line. (See following diagram.) In this instance, there is a heightening of mind with no change in will. From the model one can see that this is roughly equivalent to going back to the point on the Path where we once began our detour. In some systems of metaphysical thought, that detour point historically took place in Atlantean or early Egyptian times.

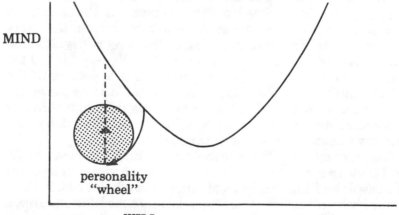

MIND

personality
"wheel"

WILL

The seeker who follows this option is most likely to be concerned with mind development. It may take the form of mind dynamics courses, parapsychological phenomena, or any disciplines which offer experiences of an expanded dimension of mind but fail to require any development of the will. Occasionally, we even find that people who pursue this course are fascinated with ancient prehistoric cultures, not for anthropological values but because of a desire to recreate states of mind that existed in these times.

One problem with this option is that again it is going back; however, not as far back as with the first option nor in so dangerous a way. In a sense, there is a familiarity to the place in consciousness which this course of seeking offers. But another problem with this second option should concern us more: this pathway largely involves a strengthening of personality patterns with no development of the individuality. Since there are no requirements for awakening the will, what we get is a higher dimensional experience of our personalities. Consider the example of a seeker who joins a mind development class. The advertisements for the class may promise experiences of "psychic ability, mentally induced prosperity, and deep alpha level meditations." In fact the participant may gain such experiences, but all of them may simply be extensions of his or her personality desires and habits.

In a fashion, this pathway has taken the seeker back to the Path, but has it left him or her in an optimal position? Probably not. With the personality traits strengthened and more entrenched, the seeker will not be likely to proceed with the development of will and individuality which is now needed. This problem is depicted on this version of the model by reconstructing a concept used earlier regarding the chief feature or chief misunderstanding of the personality. It is the hub around which the personality rotates. We can think of the detour arrow of the model as transcribing a portion of the circular pathway of the personality "wheel." In this sense, the movement of the dotted line passes directly through the hub of this wheel and is likely to be strongly influenced by this primary misunderstanding of the personality.

The third option offers the most direct and, for most people, the best way back to the Path. It is a simultaneous development of the will and higher states of mind. It is a balanced, holistic avenue which makes use of tools such as meditation, dream analysis, self-study, and physical attunement, to mention just a few. The hard work of awakening the will is inspired by experiences of higher mind. The potentially hypnotic effect of higher dimensions of mind is balanced by a strengthened will. This leads us to a point on the Path which is new. This third option is truly evolutionary because it takes us to places where the soul has not yet been. To the extent that we can speak of anyone's unique soul mission as contained within the flow of the greater Path, then this third option is the most direct way to find and live that soul purpose. The full flowering of one's soul mission lies at the points along the parabolic path which engage the fourth stage of will. But this third optional pathway back to the greater Path is seen by many as the most effective and efficient method by which to start that process.

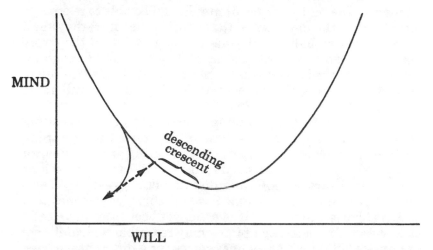

One other feature of this third pathway should be noted, because it is an experience which troubles so many seekers. Note that on the model there is a curious phenomenon which occurs. Once one has re-established a point of experiencing which is in attunement with the images and archetypes of the Path, there is a movement "downward," relatively speaking. Of course, words such as "up" and "down" are highly misleading in this case. Instead, we might describe this "descending crescent" along the parabola as a period in which the will is continuing to awaken but the mind becomes less and less inclined to provide experiences of higher dimensional reality.

Many seekers have gone through such a period in their lives—perhaps more than once, because we continually veer off the Path only to have to work our way back to It again. This "descending cescent' is a crucial stage because of the likelihood of the seeker becoming discouraged. From such discouragement, he or she may cease to seek or may resort to the first or second options instead. The mistakeK3 that is made involves equating progress along the Path with *only* the dimension of mind, forgetting that our model is two dimensional and requires a growth of will also.

During the period of the "descending crescent," life continues to present, special challenges and opportunities which shall allow the sense of individuality to emerge, but at the expense of personality. In order for this to happen effectively, a period is needed in which altered states of mind are not readily available. The higher states of mind shall be able to re-emerge further along the Path, but at that point in the future they shall serve the individuality and sense of soul mission. If they were readily available during this crucial period of the "descending crescent," they might only take one back into a false feeling of oneself and make the necessary development of will more difficult.

What does it feel like to be in a period of the "descending crescent"? It is likely to be a time in which we find it hard to meditate or to remember hopeful and inspiring dreams. It is, for many people, a time of outward failure—when the impressions brought to awareness by the mind do not suggest the health and success that one assumed would come with consistent seeking. For some people, it is a time of becoming physically sick. Even though the symptoms may resemble typical illness of physical life, such a sickness comes for a different purpose. Whatever form the "descending crescent" takes in our lives, its purpose is to bring us to the point of surrender. But surrender does not mean a "giving up motivated by doubt" but rather a "letting go based on hope." The "descending crescent" ends when we move into the realm of Real Will. At that point we have turned a corner and the developmental purpose for this classic stage in the spiritual quest has been accomplished.

Finally, we should note that there is one other option, depicted by the horizontal dotted line (see next diagram). This is an extraordinarily difficult pathway which involves just the development of the will with no expansion of the mind. Some spiritual disciplines seem to speak of such a developmental direction. Renouncing all interest or concern with higher dimensional experiences of mind, they set to work on shedding the personality and awakening the individuality through a focused awakening of the will.

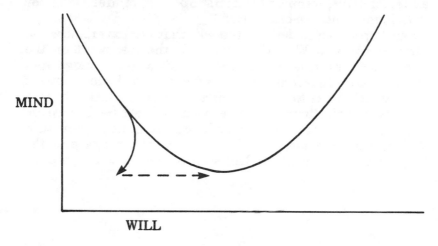

From one perspective this is the most direct pathway, because it leads to a point farthest along the great Path. However, most seekers need the periodic inspiration of higher dimensional mind experiences to keep moving along. As we can see from our model, this fourth pathway is difficult also because of its length. It involves a relatively long movement before reconnecting with the Path. In systems such as that of Gurdjieff, this pathway requires a teacher. Starting from a point with little or no will, it is difficult to imagine the seeker doing a work of sheer will development on his or her own. A constant guide who has already reached and sustained Real Will is needed. As an infrequently traveled route, this pathway lacks signposts or archetypal images which can guide or reassure the solitary traveler.

With this overall model in mind and the four basic options before us, the question naturally arises, "Where am I on the model?" The answer is not a simple point but rather many points, because each of us spends different parts of the day at different positions in relation to mind and will.

For example, most of us spend the better part of waking life in the limited state of mind we call three-dimensional consciousness and with little or no will awakened. This point has been depicted in the model as the tip of the arrow, which illustrates our detour from the Plan. But we may have moments in the day of heightened states of mind and/or increased

147

functionings of the will. As we progress on this spiritual quest, we begin to be able to spend more and more of our lives experiencing, from positions on the model, greater individuality and co-creativity.

Our hope is so to develop the will that our experiences are directed by Real Will. Once we pass the low point on the parabola's curve (the point on the will axis where we move from stage three to stage four will), then the expanded dimensions of mind which come to our awareness can be worked with in a purposeful, objective and co-creative way. It is here that we are truly in touch with the mission of our lives. Once we can "turn this corner," we are in a flow of insight, energy and the "capacity to do" which shall allow us to live our soul's purpose.

Epilogue

Discovering your soul's purpose. This is an invitation that is extended to each of us. It is a calling to find and clarify a meaning for life—a meaning that is universal and also one which is unique to each individual. However, that discovery process is an ongoing one. The way in which you relate to your mission is a continuing adventure. Even when you think you have found the essence of your soul's purpose, there is still room for an experimental approach to life in which you are always finding new ways in which that mission can be expressed.

In this book you have had the chance to get started with several specific discovery tools. Each one of these techniques has the potential to help you find what your mission is about. But each one can also be applied in an ongoing way to help you stay in closer touch with your individuality and to live your purpose more effectively.

You have examined in detail the dual perspective of your being: the personality and the individuality. Simply having that point of view available is a powerful technique for understanding life. You have also explored the Jungian notion of psychological functions which create your temperament. Your basic blueprint for perceiving and evaluating life offers certain clues for finding your mission. It also suggests the parts of yourself which may be especially burdened by habit and mechanicalness. This Jungian model implies particular ways in which you might be able to tap insights from the unconscious or be alert to influences which come from beyond material life.

The technique of self-observation or "standing aside and watching self go by" is one which you are encouraged to continue applying. Even when you think you have found your mission, you will still discover that this tool is helpful for dis-identifying from personality patterns which would keep you from living that purpose. You have also read a brief discussion of the language of the soul—nonanalytical methods of tuning in to deeper levels of understanding and purposefulness within you. Perhaps you have already begun to experiment with one or more of these approaches.

Finally, you have made a study of the human will and its highly significant role in allowing you to find and live your mission. The will is a key ingredient of your individuality center—that place in consciousness where your mission is known and from which it can be lived. By awakening your will through the various stages of its development, you are doing a work directly related to living your soul's purpose.

When you feel that your efforts to apply the concepts in this book are beginning to be fruitful, then take time to complete one further exercise. It is to write a letter to yourself, a letter from your individuality to your personality! To some people the idea of writing a letter to oneself sounds silly; and yet most people who try this kind of exercise report that it is a very moving and helpful experience. In Appendix B of this book is an outline for your letter. The letter begins with "Dear ......" and you are to fill in the name that your personality goes by. Then the letter proceeds with certain sections already written for you and other sections left for you to fill in. At the end the letter is signed "Love, mySelf," in other words, from your individuality.

Conclusions

In closing, you are asked to keep in mind three simple points as you continue to work on living the ideas in this book. First is that you are encouraged to find and live your unique mission, but not just for your private well-being. Admittedly, the living of your mission will bring a sense of personal fulfillment to you, and that is important. But perhaps even more important is the effect upon the world at large that you will have by living your soul's purpose.

The Cayce readings are not alone in promising that a relatively small number of people can have a disproportionately large impact for good. This principle is sometimes called a "threshold" or "critical mass" effect. It has been popularized by the story of the "hundredth monkey." The Cayce readings sometimes presented this same idea with the homey phrase, "A little leaven can leaven the whole lump." By whatever words the principle is expressed, it is a very significant concept related to the study of your mission in life.

How can you be among the group of people who can turn the course of events in the world today? How can you be one who contributes to a grace-ful rather than karmic unfoldment in these times of change and transition for the human family? The answer is simple: only by living your soul's mission. In other words, what is critically needed in the world today is a relatively small number of people who will find and live the purpose for which they incarnated. If this happens, then the future for all humankind may be deeply altered for the good. So, it is in this sense that you should keep in mind that the discovery and living of your soul's purpose is not merely for your own private well-being.

The second concluding point for you to keep in mind states: The Universe is on your side. This idea is at the heart of the philosophy found in the Cayce material. The Creative Forces, the universal archetypes of spiritual evolution, Life itself, all of these influences are on the side of your successful living of a mission. Each day help is offered no matter how far you have drifted from the intent of that mission. It is only you yourself who can get in the way and block the living of your soul's mission. Everything else that really counts is on the side of success.

Finally, keep in mind this principle as you continue to search for and to live your soul's purpose. Although it may seem very challenging and often stretches you to your limits, your soul's mission is something which is do-able. In wisdom, you as a soul chose something to accomplish for this incarnation. It was something that would force you to change and grow, but something that can be reached. With a feeling of joy and hopefulness, be about that mission and experience the fulfillment it will bring to you and to others.

APPENDIX A
Bibliography of Recommended Reading

Jung, C.G. *Memories, Dreams and Reflections.* Harvest Books (Random House), New York, 1961.

This fine, readable autobiography, written near the end of Jung's life, provides a beautiful narrative and "case history" of his life as an example of the individuation process.

Jung, C.G. *Modern Man in Search of a Soul.* Harcourt Brace Jovanovich, New York, 1933.

This collection of essays provides some of Jung's most direct attempts to address key issues in the spiritual quest. The first essay is an excellent summary of his compensatory approach to dream interpretation. There is an essay on psychological types; and another, particularly relevant one, entitled "Psychotherapist or Clergy?"

Ouspensky, P.D. *In Search of the Miraculous.* Harcourt Brace Jovanovich, New York, 1949.

An autographical account of Ouspensky's years with Gurdjieff, this book is perhaps the most readable of all Ouspensky's works. It also gives an excellent survey of key principles from Gurdjieff's system as seen through the eyes of what many people feel is his most brilliant student.

Speeth, Kathleen R. *The Gurdjieff Work.* Harper and Row, New York, 1976.

This is perhaps the best summary of Gurdjieff's system, written by a woman with a tremendous gift for explaining and clarifying complex subjects. A psychotherapist by profession, Speeth knew Gurdjieff personally, having spent some of her early years with her parents at Gurdjieff's Institute outside Paris.

Welch, John. *Spiritual Pilgrims.* Paulist Press, New York, 1982.

The author is a Carmelite priest who has made an extraordinary synthesis of the writings of Jung and a fellow Carmelite who lived some 400 years ago, the mystic Teresa of Avila. He uses the basic notions from Jung of individuation and archetypes to draw parallels with Teresa's stages of the inner spiritual journey. It is fascinating reading, full of practical applications for any seeker, and also provides one of the best summaries of Jungian thought.

APPENDIX B
A Letter to Yourself

Dear _____,

I need you to yield to my deep sense of purpose and mission. It is not my desire that you be removed or destroyed. But I do need your ways to become weaker and more passive as I express myself more clearly and actively.

Although it is hard to put into words the sense of purpose and mission that guides me, here are some images and glimpses of it—pieces of the puzzle—which may help you to understand:

Your cooperation is needed. Here are three habitual things in which I need you to help me become more aware and to let go of. I can even suggest some steps you might take in dealing with each one:

1.

2.

3.

Love,
mySelf

APPENDIX C
Annotated Excerpts from the Cayce Readings

Personality is necessary but individuality is more important.

When their ideals or purposes, or aims, are set aright, is as the development of an individual—and *should not* be pointed in each individual case, or else the body loses its own individuality; and *personality* is certainly something *not* to be paraded or boasted of! Well to have, and necessary! if used properly! *Without individuality,* you are nothing! 257-79

Individuality can shine through our creative acts.

Q-10. Will the entity's style be individual?

A-10. The more the entity applies self to those forces as are emanations from the Spirit. . .more *individuality* MUST be that as emanates, whether in writing, drawing, painting, or whatnot. *That's* individuality! Personality is that seen by others. Individuality is that which shines out from within, separating one from another. Though one may be but a dot, that dot remains ever individual!. . .The nearer one becomes to that which will give its *individuality*—yet losing itself in the whole—the *more* individuality one attains! 345-2

Individuality and personality defined.

Here it would be well for a discussion or interpretation of personality and individuality. Sufficient for the moment: Individuality is the soul's relationship to that as its ideal in the measures of will and desire as in accordance with what has been the ideal. Personality is that desire or purpose manifested that one desires others to see in self. . . 294-185

Influences from individuality and personality conflict.

For so oft we see contradictory effects produced in the activities of the individuality and personality of persons. 281-51

Meditation as a quickening of influences from the individuality.

As has been given, there are *definite* conditions that arise from within the inner man when an individual enters

155

into true or deep meditation. A physical condition happens, a physical activity takes place!. . .Then, changes naturally take place when there is the arousing of that stimuli *within* the individual that has within it the seat of the soul's dwelling, within the individual body of the entity or man, and then this partakes of the individuality rather than the personality.   281-13

We come into the earth with a purpose or mission.

. . .ye are to fulfill the purpose for which each soul enters the earth. . .   3333-1

For, each soul enters with a mission. . .we all have a mission to perform. . .   3003-1

Each entity, each soul, enters the material experience for purposes. These are not individual or of a selfish nature, though they are very personal in their application and their practice.   1436-1

Q-8. Is there anything in particular I can do now to accomplish the reason for present incarnation?
A-8. If there hadn't been you wouldn't be allowed to be in the earth in the present!   3051-7

Each soul as it has entered and does enter into material manifestation is to fulfill a purpose, with the Creative Forces or God. For He hath not willed that any soul should perish, but hath with every temptation, every fault, prepared a way, a manner, an opportunity for the entity to become as one with Him.   257-201

We have a free will stronger than any fate or destiny.

Q-9. Is it probable, according to a so-called spiritualist, that I will meet an elderly person who will help me in my life career towards financial success?
A-9. As indicated and given, such things should rather be builded from within. And if the soul merits such, through that it metes to its fellow man, it may bring such into the experience of the body. But to say it *will* happen—it can't be done! For, the Father Himself has given each soul that portion of Himself. What the soul does *about* his knowledge, about his abilities or opportunities, depends upon the will of the soul. Hence, as to whether this is to come to pass or may not come to pass—it may, my brother,

to *any* soul. What wilt *thou* do about the opportunities that have been and are being presented to thee? 531-3

Q-14. What value is there in palmistry? To what extent may it be relied upon?

A-14. As we have given in regard to any and every omen, it is an indication—yes. As to whether or not it will come to pass depends upon what the body, the mind of such an one does *about* that it knows in relationship to itself. It may be depended upon, then, about twenty percent as being absolute—and about eighty percent "chance" or what a body does with its opportunities.

416-2

Then, it is not that the entire life experience is laid out for an individual when there has been received that imprint as of the first breath, or the spirit entering the body as prepared for activity in the material world. For, again, choice is left to the individual, and the personality—as to whether it is the laudation of the ego or cooperation with its fellow men, or as a consecration to the service of the Creative Forces in its material environs. 281-49

Destiny defined.

Hence, *destiny* is what a soul does with *its* will as in relationship to the Creative Forces. 391-6

The reason why we have entered into material life.

First, the entering of *every* soul is that it, the soul, may become more aware or conscious of the Divine within, that the soul-body may be purged that it may be a fit companion for the glory of the Creative Forces in its activity.

518-2

Know that the purpose for which each soul enters a material experience is that it may be as a light unto others; not as one boastful of self or of self's abilities in any phase of the experience, whether mental or material, but living, being in spirit that which *is* ideal and not idealistic alone, nor the unattainable. 641-6

Hence the purposes for each soul's experience in materiality are that the Book of Remembrance may be opened that the soul may know its relationship to its Maker.

1215-4

For life in its manifestations through which the soul of an entity or body may manifest *is* purposeful, and that the individual, the soul may find its way through the vicissitudes of experience in materiality, that it may know its God.   1293-1

For all that is a part of each entity's experience is for a purpose.   1827-1

For Life is, an experience is, what each soul, each entity makes of same. Hence fulfilling that purpose as He may have in thee is a greater service, a greater joy than may be had by him who may have builded a city or have conquered a nation; for such have the greater obligations and the greater influences for their burdens.   1129-2

Daily life regularly presents us with opportunities toward soul purpose.

For *today,* in the experiences of *every* soul manifested, is the *opportunity* to make manifest that which *is* ideal, in the experience of that individual entity.   816-10

We easily misinterpret the meaning of karma and destiny.

Most individuals in the present misinterpret karmic conditions. The development or destiny as karmic influences—each soul, each entity, should gain the proper concept of destiny. Destiny is within, or is as of faith, or is as the gift of the Creative Forces. Karmic influence is, then, rebellious influence against such. When opportunities are presented, it is the entity's own *will* force that must be exercised. . .   903-23

Problems and failures can be used as stepping-stones—not just accomplishing things "in spite of" them.

In whatever state the self is found to be, *that* may be *used* as a stepping-stone to greater opportunities and to greater successes—if the laws that pertain to spiritual forces, in expression in a mental and material world, are kept in sight.   1113-1

Soul development described.

It is not the knowledge, then, but what one does with one's abilities, one's opportunities in relationships to others, that makes for the development or retardment of that individual.   1293-1

The relationship between will and other factors such as mind and desire.

Q-2. *Where does desire originate?*
A-2. Will.   262-62

But as we find, there is no greater influence than the will of an entity, that which is indeed the birthright to each soul. For with it (the will) one becomes a coordinant, cooperative factor with Creative Forces we know as God, or else becomes self-indulgent, self-glorifying, self-exalting. . .
                                                1215-4

APPENDIX D

Excerpts from the Cayce Readings on the Will

The ability to choose is WILL; as well as the ability to allow self to be used by influences. 1608-1

And what makes for the change? *Will!* What, then, is *will*? That which makes for the dividing line between the finite and the Infinite, the Divine and the wholly human, the carnal and the spiritual. For the *will* may be made one *with* HIM, or for self alone. With the will, then, does man destine in the activities of a material experience how he shall make for the relationships with truth. 262-81

Mind is the factor that is in direct opposition of will. Mind being that control of, or being the spark of the Maker, the WILL, the individual when we reach the plane of man. 3744-1

Each should know this: That as is self's own ideal is the standard by which the will is controlled or measured. 262-9

Taking count of self, and application of the will—is the developer or the retarder in earth's experiences. 5-2

For, will is that factor in the experience of each soul that determines whether it has responded to that it has set as its ideal such as to make for developments along those lines, or whether retardments have been the experience of such a soul-entity. 510-1

For the WILL of an individual is the MOTIVATIVE force; that is, that which makes for the choice which is made by the individual under this or that circumstance, this or that experience. 5747-2

For fear is—as it ever has been—that influence that opposes will, and yet fear is only of the moment while will is of eternity. Hence fear takes hold upon the emotions, while will is deeper-seated into the soul, into the warp and woof of the very being of an *entity* in its entirety. . . 1210-1

. . .by the application of will, which makes of man that difference between man and the rest of creation. . . 240-2

. . .*will* is that factor that is the pivot upon which the soul of man may make his body-soul one with the Father or turn into self-indulgences, self-aggrandizements that bring detrimental forces in the experience. 504-3

For to the entity also we would give, *know* that *will* supersedes those influences that may express themselves even as material desires; and certainly supersedes those influences that may be had from sojourns in the earth. 1210-1

While these influences appear, and innately give many an urge to an entity, there is *no influence* beyond the *will* of an entity... 2673-1

...bring self to that way of applying will wherein the Builder (the Mind) may be guided aright, and that way leads to the mark of the higher calling... 2904-1

Q-6. What is the difference between the desire of the heart and the desire of the will? And is it not possible for harmonious coordination of these? How may it be attained?
A-6. ...The heart is ordinarily considered the seat of life in the physical, while the will as a motivative factor in the mental and spiritual realm. To be sure, these may be made one.
262-64

As has been given, this is the choice, as makes God God—that His creatures are, of their own will, to be made one with the ideal as is set before them, or to conform to ideals as they themselves build. Hence the variations in human experiences—but the heritage of man is self-will. That made one *with* God is creative. That made in opposition is destructive. 254-51

...the *will* is the mainspring of existence. 97-2

For the will of each entity, of each soul, is that which individualizes it, makes it aware of itself... 853-9

As to what an entity does concerning its environs...from the *material* viewpoint, this is governed by the action of the will (that active principle making for the *individuality* of an entity...). Thus is *man* endowed with the individual soul.
Hence the *will* is an *attribute* of the soul, and the whole development of an entity. 274-1

What Is A.R.E.?

The Association for Research and Enlightenment, Inc. (A.R.E.®), is the international headquarters for the work of Edgar Cayce (1877-1945), who is considered the best-documented psychic of the twentieth century. Founded in 1931, the A.R.E. consists of a community of people from all walks of life and spiritual traditions, who have found meaningful and life-transformative insights from the readings of Edgar Cayce.

Although A.R.E. headquarters is located in Virginia Beach, Virginia—where visitors are always welcome—the A.R.E. community is a global network of individuals who offer conferences, educational activities, and fellowship around the world. People of every age are invited to participate in programs that focus on such topics as holistic health, dreams, reincarnation, ESP, the power of the mind, meditation, and personal spirituality.

In addition to study groups and various activities, the A.R.E. offers membership benefits and services, a bimonthly magazine, a newsletter, extracts from the Cayce readings, conferences, international tours, a massage school curriculum, an impressive volunteer network, a retreat-type camp for children and adults, and A.R.E. contacts around the world. A.R.E. also maintains an affiliation with Atlantic University, which offers a master's degree program in Transpersonal Studies.

For additional information about A.R.E. activities hosted near you, please contact:

A.R.E.
67th St. and Atlantic Ave.
P.O. Box 595
Virginia Beach, VA 23451-0595
(804) 428-3588

A.R.E. Press

A.R.E. Press is a publisher and distributor of books, audiotapes, and videos that offer guidance for a more fulfilling life. Our products are based on, or are compatible with, the concepts in the psychic readings of Edgar Cayce.

For a free catalog, please write to A.R.E. Press at the address below or call toll free 1-800-723-1112. For any other information, please call 804-428-3588.

A.R.E. Press
Sixty-Eighth & Atlantic Avenue
P.O. Box 656
Virginia Beach, VA 23451-0656